HOW THE ENVIRONMENT WORKS

HOW THE ENVIRONMENT WORKS

PRESTON GRALLA

Illustrated by
CHERIE PLUMLEE

Ziff-Davis Press
Emeryville, California

Development Editor	Valerie Haynes Perry
Copy Editor	Kelly Green
Technical Reviewers	Dr. Lynn Epstein and Dr. Daniel Bromberger
Project Coordinator	Cort Day
Proofreader	Carol Burbo
Cover Illustration	Cherie Plumlee
Cover Design	Regan Honda
Book Design	Carrie English
Technical Illustration	Cherie Plumlee Computer Graphics and Illustration
Word Processing	Howard Blechman
Page Layout	Tony Jonick
Indexer	Valerie Haynes Perry

Ziff-Davis Press books are produced on a Macintosh computer system with the following applications: FrameMaker®, Microsoft® Word, QuarkXPress®, Adobe Illustrator®, Adobe Photoshop®, Adobe Streamline™, MacLink®*Plus*, Aldus® FreeHand™, Collage Plus™.

If you have comments or questions or would like to receive a free catalog, call or write:
Ziff-Davis Press
5903 Christie Avenue
Emeryville, CA 94608
1-800-688-0448

ISBN 1-56276-232-X

Manufactured in the United States of America
✪ This book is printed on paper that contains 50% total recycled fiber of which 20% is de-inked postconsumer fiber.
10 9 8 7 6 5 4 3 2 1

For Gabriel and Mia,
whose sense of wonder
and endless questions per-
meate every page of this
book. And for Lydia, who
made it all possible.

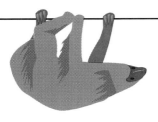

Freshwater: The Stream of Life
135

The Energy Conundrum
155

The Ecology of Man-Made Environments
179

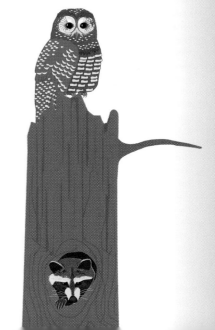

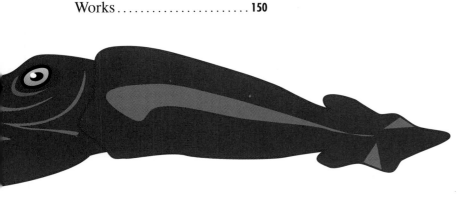

The creation of any book is by necessity a group effort, and this book was more of one than most. First I'd like to thank the countless environmental groups and government officials who lent me their time at no charge. The library of the Environmental Protection Agency in Boston was of notable aid.

In doing research, I relied on many books. *The World Environment 1972–1992* published by Chapman & Hall on behalf of the United Nations Environment Programme, was of vital help, as was the *State of the World 1994, a Worldwatch Institute Report on Progress Toward a Sustainable Society*, published by W.W Norton & Company. *Earth in the Balance* by now Vice President Al Gore, published by Plume, gave an excellent overview of environmental issues, while *Healing the Planet*, by Paul and Anne Ehrlich, provided the scientific and philosophical underpinning for it all.

Particular thanks goes to everyone at Ziff-Davis Press. I especially want thank Cindy Hudson, who had the faith to entrust the project to me, and Cheryl Holzaepfel, for working on the outline and making sure it all made sense, and Eric Stone, whose regular phone calls assuaged the sense of being somewhere off in the wilderness, which is a sentiment that many authors share. Development editor Valerie Haynes Perry was a godsend: In her gentle but firm way she managed to delete the bad writing and add the good, as well as keeping the entire project moving along and bolstering my spirits with her well-timed compliments. Cherie Plumlee, technical illustrator, accomplished the seemingly impossible: She turned my chicken-scrawl drawings into remarkable illustrations that do more than simply convey information: They are beautiful works in themselves. Technical reviewers Dr. Lynn Epstein and Dr. Daniel Bromberger are to be thanked for correcting any mistakes in chemistry, biology, and environmental science. Kelly Green, copy editor, always made my writing seem better than it really was. Cort Day, project coordinator, somehow managed to juggle all the disparate elements and was responsible for actually turning this into a book. Tony Jonick, layout artist, helped make this the beautiful book that it is. And Carol Burbo, proofreader, and Howard Blechman, word processor, somehow managed to get all the scribblings and handwritten notes straight and the text right.

And of course, the biggest thanks of all goes to my wife Lydia, who put up with lost weekends for too many months. Hey, Lyd: I'm free now! Let's get a babysitter and have a night on the town.

Subdue it [the earth]; and have dominion over the fish of the sea and the fowl of the air and over every living thing that moveth.

—The Book of Genesis

The earth does not belong to man; man belongs to the earth. All things are connected, like the blood that unites us all. Man did not weave the web of life; he is merely a strand in it. Whatever he does to the web he does to himself.

—Sentiments attributed to Chief Seattle
(Joseph Campell, *Transformations of the Myth through Time*,
Vol. 1, *The Soul of the Ancients*)

Up until the middle part of this century, most Americans may have interpreted the first quote to mean that the earth was created explicitly for our pleasure and exploitation, and that we could use its boundless resources endlessly, with few consequences.

This was before we began to see evidence of the environmental devastation that this outlook condones. It was before we recognized how badly we had fouled our air and water and land and sky. It was before environmental catastrophes resulted in casualties, as in the Chernobyl disaster, and before the slow accumulation of waste and pollution caused slow death by diseases. It was before much of our wild land and animals had vanished.

On the other hand, environmentalists have told us for some time that we should view ourselves as strands within the vast web of the earth. It's only now that we're beginning to listen to them.

This book is for anyone who wants to listen. Everyone *talks* about the environment, but who really *knows* how it works? Hopefully, you will after reading this book. It's generally politics, not the environment, that people talk about: whether the spotted owl should be protected; whether industries should be allowed greater leeway in polluting; whether nuclear power plants should be built. This book bypasses political debate, and instead looks at how this vast, interconnected web of our earth works, how miraculously every living thing—and nonliving thing—fits together. It will show, for example, how the spotted owl is intimately tied to the forests in which it lives. It will explain why the rain forests are important to everyone on the planet, not just those living near them.

Through text and graphics, this book will take you on a guided tour of all the major aspects of our environment. It starts by giving an overall view of the earth as a single ecosystem, and covers the biology and chemistry underlying how all life works on earth—that is, how the nitrogen, carbon, and oxygen cycles transform the energy of the sun and the nutrients in the soil into all living matter. Then it covers, in turn, how every part of the living earth—what is called the biosphere—works, from the rain forest to the depths of the ocean to our rivers, streams, land, and sky.

The book does more than that, though: It also portrays the environmental damage we have caused in our attempts to exploit the earth's many resources. It details causative factors such as the precise chemical reactions that contribute to the depletion of the ozone layer, oil spills, and sick building syndrome.

You will learn about the two main causes of environmental devastation: overpopulation and reliance on nonrenewable energy sources. Ecologists use a term—*carrying capacity*—to refer to the largest given population that can be supported by a given ecosystem. When an ecosystem's carrying capacity is exceeded, the effect is an adverse impact on the environment. There are those who believe that we have exceeded the earth's carrying capacity. Most of our woes are caused by overpopulation: Everything from air and water pollution to the manmade creation of deserts has its roots in overpopulation.

Overreliance on nonrenewable, polluting sources of energy is the other primary cause of environmental problems that is discussed in this book. Coal and oil are the two most notable examples that fall into this category. Acid rain, global warming, and smog are just three examples of this.

Perhaps most importantly of all, this book doesn't just portray the problems—it illustrates solutions as well. You will see how solar and wind energy can be created, how oil spills are cleaned, how sewage is treated, and more.

In writing this book, I have hoped that as more people understand more about how the environment works, they will also recognize how fragile it is. Our instincts should call for its protection, so that this great green earth of ours will be here to enjoy forever.

A GLOBAL VIEW

CONTENTS

FROM THE HUMBLEST one-celled bacteria to the most sophisticated lifeform of all—humankind—all life on earth is connected by a vast, almost incomprehensibly complex web. Touch one part and the whole vibrates; cut one thread and the entire web is threatened with collapse. This web is called an ecosystem.

Not only does an ecosystem link all life-forms; it also connects *abiotic*, or non-living, elements. Sunlight, water, air, gases, minerals, and the earth beneath our feet are all examples of abiotic elements within an ecosystem. In fact, just about everything the eye can see, and much that it cannot, is inextricably conjoined.

These life-forms and abiotic elements are bound together by elaborate biological and chemical processes. Geological and climatological factors also come into play. All of these processes together form what environmentalists call the biosphere—the thin layer of air, land, water, and living things that supports life on earth. As seen from outer space, the biosphere appears eggshell-thin, poised precipitously between the emptiness of space and the stoniness of the planet beneath it. However, to us within the biosphere the layer seems impossibly large: We look in one direction and see endless land, and in another direction we see endless ocean. We look above and see boundless sky.

The interdependent relationships between all life-forms and nonliving things within the biosphere are so complex that some scientists look at the earth as if it were a single organism. This somewhat controversial theory is called the Gaia hypothesis, named after Gaia, the ancient Greek goddess of the earth. However, there is no doubt that the entire biosphere is changed when you alter just one of its components.

Humankind has altered the biosphere significantly in countless ways. Unfortunately, these changes have generally been for the worse. We have practically monopolized the earth's food chain, have destroyed countless species of plants and animals, and have affected just about every aspect of the way the ecosystem works. We've influenced everything from the way that forests regulate the water cycle, to how wetlands filter pollutants and how the ozone layer filters out dangerous ultraviolet rays.

It is important to keep in mind the concept of carrying capacity when thinking of the earth as a whole, or any ecosystem within it. *Carrying capacity* refers to the largest number of individuals and species that a habitat can support indefinitely. There is no doubt that we have begun to exceed the carrying capacity for parts of the earth. Our gobbling of resources and spewing of wastes cannot go on forever, or we'll risk exceeding the carrying capacity of the planet.

However, we can fix what we have done. We will have to keep in mind some important basic environmental principles in order to accomplish this. These principles apply to virtually every aspect of the world's ecosystem. First, we must realize that we are dependent upon the earth's resources every second of our lives. These resources can be biological, such as plants and animals we eat, or microorganisms that perform vital biochemical processes. The resources can also be abiotic, such as gases, water, soil, and minerals.

We must also keep in mind that all animals and humans consume resources—and these resources are finite. Though we like to think otherwise, the earth's resources are not limitless. For this reason, solving environmental woes requires a stabilization of population growth. Since there's a limit to the earth's resources and to how much waste can be recycled, unless population growth is halted, the problems cannot be resolved. However, some resources, such as crops, trees, and other plant products, are renewable. And if they are handled properly, they can become self-sustaining. Other resources—fossil fuels such as coal and oil, for example—are nonrenewable; they can be used up.

Energy is an important and limited resource. We need energy in the form of food—plants and other animals. But we need energy in other forms as well—to heat homes, drive factories, and power automobiles, for example.

Environmental problems result from consuming resources at unsustainable levels and producing waste that cannot be biodegraded and recycled. People in developed countries consume a much greater amount of resources and produce much more waste than those in undeveloped countries. Because of this, developed countries cause a good portion—though not all—of the world's environmental problems. However, environmental problems are international problems. Dirty air and polluted water do not stop at a country's border. In order to solve these problems, we have to change the way we use resources and produce waste. The goal is to use resources so they will last forever. And we must produce waste in a form and at a rate that the biosphere can handle without being harmed.

As you read this book, keep these principles in mind. Not only will they guide you in understanding how the environment works, they will also show you how we can save it.

The chapters in this section look at how the biosphere functions. They cover everything from a global view of how the living planet functions, to an examination of the basic chemical cycles that make all life possible. You'll also see how we're destroying the earth's balance—and examine some ways in which we're trying to restore to the earth what we've already taken from it.

The Earth as an Ecosystem

THE SUN IS THE source of all life. Its massive heat engine drives our entire biosphere. Solar radiation heats the biosphere, warming it enough to support life. Solar radiation also provides the energy to set in motion a variety of chemical and physical processes that form the biosphere's life-support systems.

Our atmosphere filters the sun's energy. The atmosphere reflects about 30% of the sun's heat off into space. The rest of this energy makes its way toward earth and heats the air, land, and water. This same energy also creates ocean currents, wind, and our weather; it even sets in motion the water cycle that circulates water throughout the earth. The atmosphere's ozone layer also protects us from ultraviolet rays.

The food chain is the means by which every living thing recycles energy from the sun. This chain starts with plants. Plants convert sunlight into living matter via photosynthesis. *Photosynthesis* is the process by which plants take minerals, gases, and other raw materials from the soil and air, and use the energy in sunlight to convert those materials into living, organic matter. This organic matter forms the bottom of the biosphere's vast food chain. Some animals eat plants, other animals eat the plant-eaters, and when the animals die, bacteria and microorganisms convert them into nutrients that plants can use.

However, humankind has corrupted this cycle. Scientists provide some sobering facts about ways in which we've disrupted the food chain. They estimate that before the advent of human beings, the earth's ecosystem had the potential of producing some 150 billion tons of organic matter each year. Scientists estimate that we have already destroyed about 12% of that capacity. They also say we use another 27% of the total. This means that one single species has taken up almost 40% of the entire planet's potential food supply and that all other plant and animal species are essentially on a starvation diet.

Clearly, this kind of destruction and consumption cannot go on forever if the biosphere is to survive. When we tear down forests, we're destroying the bottom of the food chain. This means creatures higher on the chain—including us—suffer the ultimate harm. And as we overpopulate the world and consume more and more resources, we monopolize the food chain, potentially leading to its final collapse.

We must consume resources at levels that can be sustained forever. This is our only assurance that we will be able to maintain the kind of life that we and our children want to live.

The Global Ecosystem

1 The sun is the engine that drives Earth. The heat and light that the sun generates travel as solar radiation some 93 million miles through space. The sun's heat blankets the earth, making it warm enough for living things to thrive. This same heat powers the biochemical reactions necessary to sustain life. The sun's energy flows through every living thing via the process of photosynthesis. In essence, we are all recycled sunlight.

2 When sunlight hits the atmosphere, some 30% of it is reflected back out into space. Nearly half of it goes to heat the atmosphere, the land, and the sea. Nearly one quarter of this sunlight sets in motion the water cycle, the winds, and the ocean currents. Plants use a tiny 0.02% for photosynthesis. In the process of photosynthesis, plants take the energy of the sun, nutrients from the soil, gases from the air, and water, and convert them all into living plant matter.

3 Carbon dioxide, water vapor, and other gases in the atmosphere absorb some of the sun's heat that is reflected off the earth's surface. These gases radiate the heat back toward the ground, warming the earth and acting as a blanket. A layer of ozone in the atmosphere acts as a sunscreen against harmful ultraviolet rays.

8 Carnivores, such as weasels, lions, foxes, and owls, eat the herbivores. *Omnivores*, such as humans, eat both plants and animals. There are often two types of carnivores in a food chain—primary carnivores and secondary carnivores. A primary carnivore, such as a weasel, feeds upon an herbivore, such as a mouse. A secondary carnivore, such as a bobcat, feeds on primary carnivores.

4 When the sun's energy reaches the earth it sets in motion a vast, global water cycle. The sun evaporates water from oceans, lakes, and rivers into the atmosphere. This water condenses into clouds, which then produce rain and snow. After the rain falls, it flows as surface runoff into rivers and lakes. It also seeps through rocks and is stored in underground aquifers. The water then flows into the ocean from rivers and aquifers, and the water cycle begins again.

9 When plants, carnivores, and other animals die, microorganisms such as bacteria and fungi break them down and extract nutrients from them. These microorganisms return the nutrients to the soil, where plants use them to begin the food chain again.

5 When sunlight strikes plants, it starts the food chain that nourishes all life on the planet. The food chain is a pyramid that rarely goes beyond four or five levels (called trophic levels). At the bottom there are large numbers of small organisms. As you move up the chain, there are fewer organisms, but each one tends to be larger. Energy is lost at each stage of the food chain; only about 10% to 20% of the energy gets transferred up to the next level. Thus, the shorter the food chain, the more energy is made available. This is why fewer resources are required to feed vegetarians than meat-eaters.

7 Herbivores—animals such as rabbits, mice, and cows—feed on the plants. These plant-eaters are responsible for transferring energy from the plant to the animal kingdom.

6 Plants, or *autotrophs*, are the food creators in the chain. They form the very bottom of the food chain, and are the base upon which all life is built.

Nature's Chemistry Lab

THE ENTIRE LIFE of the biosphere depends on a complex series of invisible, exquisitely balanced, and interrelated chemical reactions. They use the power of the sun to take gases from the air and nutrients from the soil, and they cycle the resulting energy and chemical compounds through all plants and animals on the earth. These reactions are known as biogeochemical cycles. They provide energy, nutrients, and the basic building blocks of life for all living matter. Biogeochemical cycles affect everything from the smallest microorganism to the most massive mammal to the makeup of the air itself.

The elements nitrogen, carbon, and oxygen are vital to life. Nitrogen is a component of biologically important compounds such as proteins, DNA, and RNA. Carbon is an essential element in biological molecules, including carbohydrates, proteins, fats, and nucleic acids. Oxygen is required for respiration, to provide plants and animals with energy.

So it shouldn't be surprising to learn that the nitrogen cycle, the carbon cycle, and the oxygen cycle are the most important biogeochemical cycles. Nitrogen, carbon, and oxygen circulate endlessly through the biosphere. Photosynthesis is important to all three cycles. In the process of photosynthesis, plants use chlorophyll and the sun's energy in chemical reactions that create living plant matter. Water, carbon from the air in the form of carbon dioxide, and nitrogen and other compounds from the soil are components of these chemical reactions.

We have done much to upset the balance of these cycles, and always with dire consequences. For example, the nitrogen-rich fertilizers used by farmers are washed from the fields by rain, and so make their way into streams, ponds, rivers, and lakes. The nitrogen stimulates the growth of algae and bacteria. The bacteria consume oxygen in the water, and the end result is the death of aquatic life.

Even more dangerous is the way we've upset the carbon and oxygen cycles. By burning fossil fuels such as oil and coal, we release an estimated 5 billion tons of carbon dioxide annually into the atmosphere. Some of that is absorbed by microscopic life in the ocean called phytoplankton, but much of it remains in the atmosphere. The destruction of huge amounts of vegetation each year, especially in rainforests, upsets the cycle even further. Rainforests normally take massive amounts of carbon dioxide out of the atmosphere and release oxygen during photosynthesis. As the forests are destroyed, they can no longer recycle carbon dioxide. The result of all this is the buildup in the atmosphere of carbon dioxide, the major culprit in global warming.

We like to think of ourselves as masters of the earth, but the truth is, we cannot escape our chemical ancestry. Only by first recognizing the ways in which we affect the most basic chemical cycles will we be able to solve some of our most dangerous environmental problems.

The Nitrogen, Carbon, and Oxygen Cycles

The Nitrogen Cycle

Nitrogen is vital to all life. It is a component of amino acids, proteins, DNA, and RNA. Although nitrogen makes up approximately 80% of the atmosphere, animals and plants cannot directly make use of it in its gaseous state (N_2). They require it to be in the form of water-soluble ammonium (NH_4^+) or nitrate (NO_3^-).

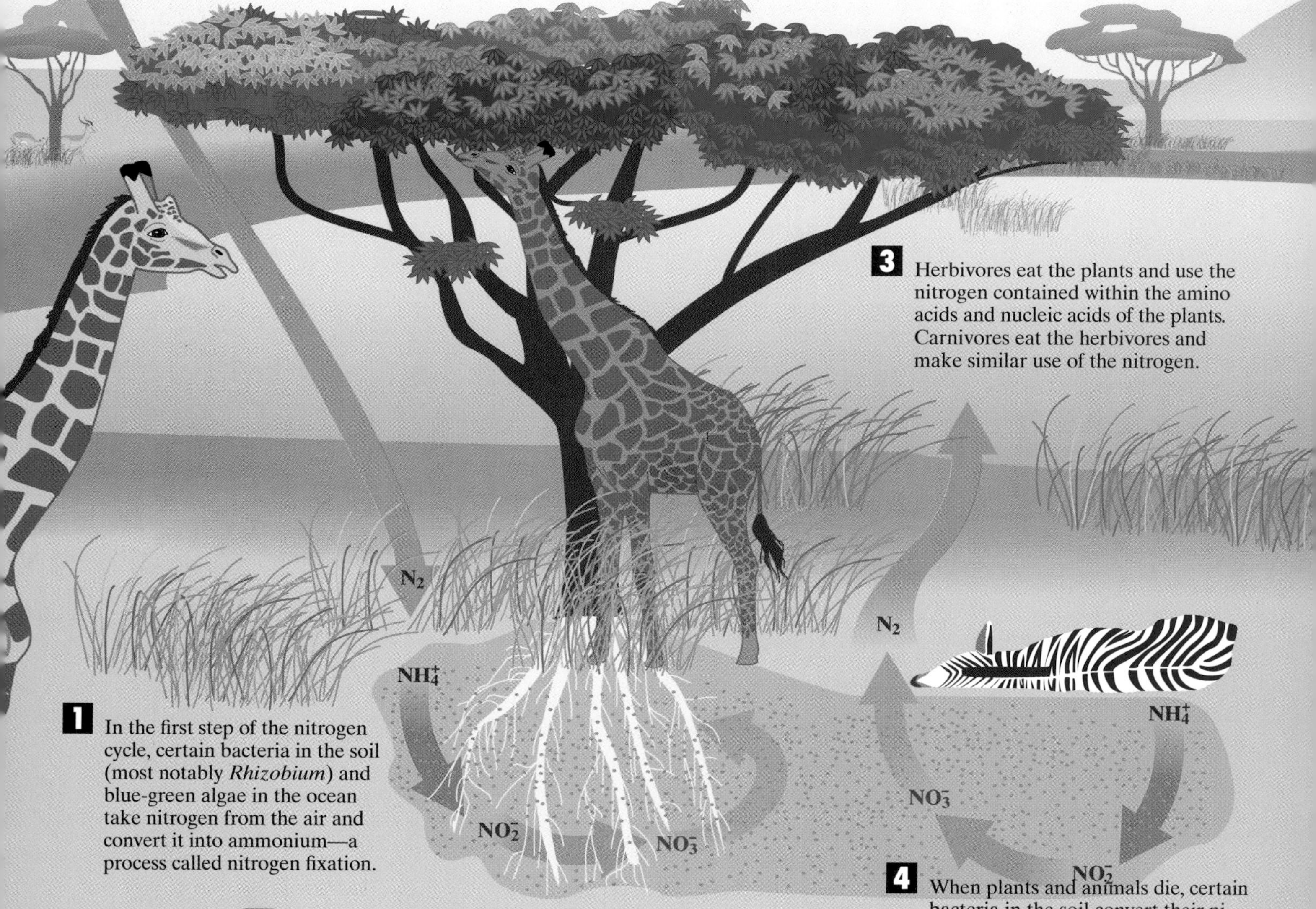

N_2

3 Herbivores eat the plants and use the nitrogen contained within the amino acids and nucleic acids of the plants. Carnivores eat the herbivores and make similar use of the nitrogen.

N_2

N_2

NH_4^+

NH_4^+

1 In the first step of the nitrogen cycle, certain bacteria in the soil (most notably *Rhizobium*) and blue-green algae in the ocean take nitrogen from the air and convert it into ammonium—a process called nitrogen fixation.

NO_2^-

NO_3^-

NO_3^-

NO_2^-

2 Some plants can use ammonium directly as a nitrogen source. Bacteria convert ammonium first into nitrites (NO_2^-), then into nitrates (NO_3^-), which plants also use for necessary compounds such as proteins, DNA, and RNA.

4 When plants and animals die, certain bacteria in the soil convert their nitrogenous compounds into nitrogen gas in a process called denitrification. The gas can now be converted by other bacteria into ammonium, and the nitrogen cycle starts all over again.

The Carbon and Oxygen Cycles

The interrelated carbon and oxygen cycles provide all plants and animals with the energy they need to live, as well as with the basic chemical building blocks of life. Carbon and oxygen, along with nitrogen and hydrogen, are the basic components of all important biological molecules. Carbon, in particular, is the key component of all organic compounds.

2 Plants release large amounts of oxygen (O_2) into the atmosphere during photosynthesis.

1 At the beginning of the photosynthesis cycle, plants use water (H_2O) and carbon dioxide (CO_2) to build carbon into simple sugars and large carbohydrates such as starch and cellulose. The plants then use the energy in the carbohydrates to oxidize the carbon they contain, transforming the carbon back into CO_2. During this respiration process, plants consume oxygen.

3 Animals eat plants and use oxygen from the air to break down the plants' carbon-based starches and sugars. This provides them with energy. Animals breathe out carbon dioxide as a waste, which plants then use during photosynthesis, beginning both cycles again.

When the Rain Comes: The Water Cycle

OVER 750 YEARS ago the Japanese author Kamo no Chomei wrote, "The flow of the river is ceaseless and its water is never the same." He thus expressed in literary terms the most basic fact about water: It is in unending motion, constantly being cycled from ocean to sky to land and back again. As it flows, plants, animals, and people use it for vital biological processes, and people also use it in agriculture, manufacturing, and recreation.

The cycle starts when water evaporates from the oceans and forms into clouds. Most of the water falls back into the ocean, but some makes its way to land. On land, water evaporates from surface waters such as lakes and rivers, and plants transpire water into the air. (*Transpiration* occurs when water evaporates from plant surfaces, especially from surface openings in the leaves.) The evaporated water then falls on land as rain, snow, and other precipitation.

When rain falls, some of it runs off into rivers and lakes and eventually makes its way to the ocean. Other water remains in the soil, where it is taken up by plants or released slowly into rivers and lakes. Still other water percolates deep underground, into vast aquifers. In areas where forest has been cut and vegetation cleared, there are no roots in the soil to hold the water. This leads to erosion and often to flooding as well.

Water seems an endlessly abundant resource, but in fact very little of it is usable. Some 97.2% of the water on the earth is salty ocean water, and so cannot be used readily. Approximately 77% of the remaining 2.8% is locked up in glaciers and ice sheets, leaving a total of only 0.65% of the earth's water available to plants, animals, and people. Though there is such a small amount of water we can use, we do not treat it with care: Water pollution of all kinds is endemic.

For example, the Rhine River supplies drinking water for approximately 30 million people, but it is so polluted that some people call it Europe's largest sewer. And in many developing countries, clean drinking water is all but impossible to find, and so millions of people—especially young children—die of waterborne diseases such as dysentery.

Making sure that everyone has an abundant supply of clean, fresh water is one of the most difficult tasks that face us. It means not only cutting down on pollution and reducing water consumption—it also means intelligent land management. Unless we face the problem now, even less of the 0.65% of the potentially usable fresh water on Earth will be potable.

The Water Cycle

1 The oceans hold almost all of the 330 million cubic miles of water on the earth—over 97%—and that is where the water cycle begins. The sun heats the ocean, evaporating water into the air—approximately 100,000 cubic miles of it each year (no salt is evaporated). The water condenses into clouds. As the clouds travel, rain, snow, and other precipitation falls. About 90% falls back into the ocean, and the remaining 10% falls onto land.

2 Over the land, more moisture is added to the air and to the clouds. This happens as water evaporates from surface water in lakes, rivers, and streams, and as vegetation transpires water into the air. Approximately 15,000 cubic miles of water makes its way into the air every year in this manner.

3 Precipitation falls over the land. When rain falls on vege-
tated areas, the soil holds in the water, which is slowly released into lakes and streams and is used by plants. Plants
require a continuous column of water to flow from their
roots to the surface of their leaves to keep them from wilt-
ing and dying. They also need water for photosynthesis.
Water travels to the leaves' surfaces and is transpired back
into the atmosphere. Other water runs off into lakes and
streams, eventually making its way back into the ocean.

5 When rain falls on areas where forests and other
vegetation have been cleared, it washes away the
topsoil, because roots are no longer present and so
do not help hold water in the soil. Roots also anchor
the soil so that it cannot be washed away. Flooding
can result from heavy rains because most of the
water that falls runs immediately into rivers and
lakes. Lakes and streams can become silted up because of the topsoil washing into them, which can
lead to further flooding. *Silting* occurs when topsoil
washes into lakes and streams, filling them with sand
and soil. This doesn't allow water to be drained to
the ocean properly, and leads to flooding.

4 Water that plants don't use, or
that does not flow into rivers
and streams, percolates through
the ground. During percolation
many pollutants are removed.
Permeable rock, such as sandstone, allows this water to form
giant underground reservoirs
called *aquifers*. The level at
which the reservoir is located
is called the water table. Deep
underground, water stored in
aquifers slowly flows back into
the ocean.

Water table

How We Cause Environmental Damage

WE HAVE POISONED just about every corner of our planet, from the depths of the ocean, to the far reaches of the land, to the very top of the sky. Toxic chemicals, organic wastes, poisonous gases…the litany of what we spew into the water, land, and sky can go on endlessly.

The health effects are known only too well: cancer, leukemia, and diseases of the lung among many others. But we have done more than endanger our health—we have also altered just about every aspect of the biosphere.

The ways in which we pollute the planet are varied, but the causes can be stated quite simply. We consume too much. We reuse too little. We produce some wastes that can't be recycled, and we don't do enough to recycle those wastes that can be reused.

Much of this is attributable to population growth. When there are too many people, we use resources at too fast a rate. But our view of the earth is also a contributing factor. We see the earth as an endless resource that can never be used up. Although the earth can replenish itself, given time and the proper treatment, we have given it neither time nor suitable care.

On the water and land, much of our pollution is caused by industrial processes, and by the very act of living. Industry produces some waste that is not properly recycled or disposed of. We cause similar problems in our homes: Everything from household chemicals to sewage ends up in our groundwater, lakes, rivers, and streams. It's true that our air is filled with gases and chemicals spewn from smokestacks—but it's also filled with similar chemicals produced by our automobiles.

To stop this we have to design a society in which we consume natural resources at the same rate at which they replenish themselves. Energy and its wastes must be handled more intelligently. We rely far too much on nonrenewable, polluting fuels, especially fossil fuels such as coal and oil. We must look toward alternative forms of energy, such as the sun and the wind. We must limit population growth and find ways to reuse or break down wastes. And we need to develop industries and pattern our lives in such a way that we produce less waste in the first place.

Finally, we all have to take some personal responsibility. Many cities and towns have voluntary or mandatory recycling programs, and we all need to take these efforts seriously. We also should buy more goods that are produced from recycled materials, and that use as few resources as possible. As the saying goes, "Think globally, but act locally." In these small ways, we can all help save the planet.

How We Pollute the Land and Air

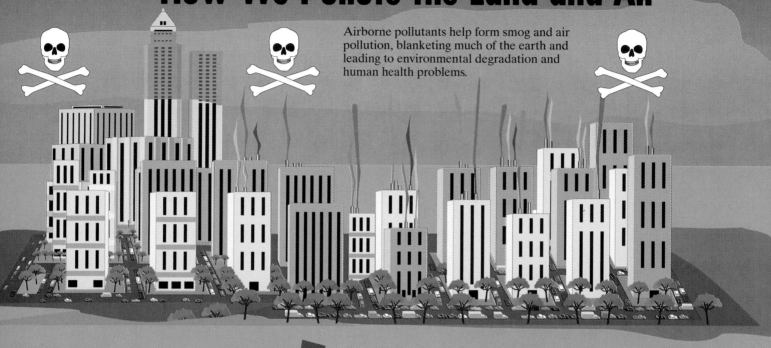

Airborne pollutants help form smog and air pollution, blanketing much of the earth and leading to environmental degradation and human health problems.

Nuclear power plants produce nuclear waste of various kinds, ranging from dangerous, high-level radioactive material that will stay radioactive for thousands of years, to less toxic substances. Vast amounts of nuclear waste are created every year. According to one estimate, the ten top nuclear energy nations will create more than 25,000 cubic meters of high-level radioactive waste over the next 30 years. That waste is now in temporary storage, because no long-range solution to storing it has been found. Less publicized than this kind of waste are the tons of lower-level radioactive wastes produced in the mining and processing of uranium before it is used for fuel.

Factories, automobiles, electricity-generating plants, and homes burn fossil fuels, which release the gases carbon dioxide, sulfur dioxide, and nitrogen dioxide, as well as many other airborne pollutants.

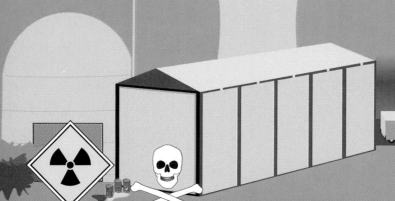

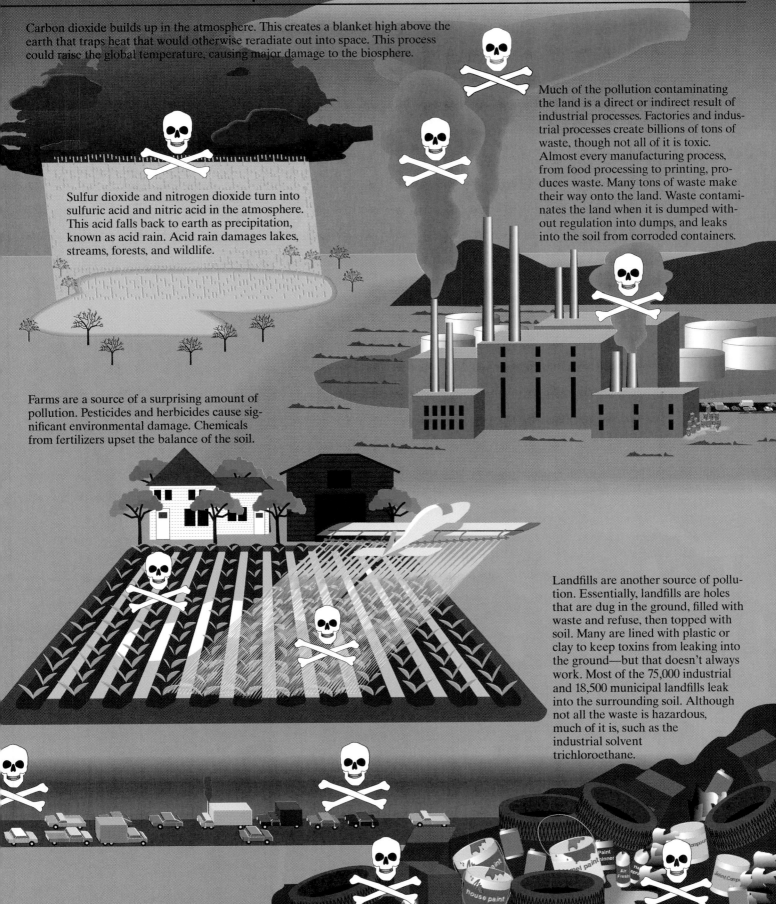

Carbon dioxide builds up in the atmosphere. This creates a blanket high above the earth that traps heat that would otherwise reradiate out into space. This process could raise the global temperature, causing major damage to the biosphere.

Much of the pollution contaminating the land is a direct or indirect result of industrial processes. Factories and industrial processes create billions of tons of waste, though not all of it is toxic. Almost every manufacturing process, from food processing to printing, produces waste. Many tons of waste make their way onto the land. Waste contaminates the land when it is dumped without regulation into dumps, and leaks into the soil from corroded containers.

Sulfur dioxide and nitrogen dioxide turn into sulfuric acid and nitric acid in the atmosphere. This acid falls back to earth as precipitation, known as acid rain. Acid rain damages lakes, streams, forests, and wildlife.

Farms are a source of a surprising amount of pollution. Pesticides and herbicides cause significant environmental damage. Chemicals from fertilizers upset the balance of the soil.

Landfills are another source of pollution. Essentially, landfills are holes that are dug in the ground, filled with waste and refuse, then topped with soil. Many are lined with plastic or clay to keep toxins from leaking into the ground—but that doesn't always work. Most of the 75,000 industrial and 18,500 municipal landfills leak into the surrounding soil. Although not all the waste is hazardous, much of it is, such as the industrial solvent trichloroethane.

How We Pollute Water

Industries are a major source of water pollution. Chemicals from waste treatment plants can leak into the groundwater and be discharged into waterways. Holding ponds for chemical wastes can also leak into groundwater. Chemical wastes, oil, and other dangerous substances are sometimes kept in underground storage tanks, and these sometimes leak into the groundwater as well. Wastes may even be directly discharged into waterways without any treatment whatsoever. This is especially true in developing countries.

Precipitation can carry pollutants, which make their way into lakes and streams. Most notably, acid rain has been destroying much water life in the eastern United States and eastern Canada, as well as in the Scandanavian countries.

Hazardous wastes such as oven cleaners and paint thinners are generated in homes and apartment buildings. These wastes make their way into our water supply and waterways.

Septic systems pollute both groundwater and surface water. An estimated 1 trillion gallons of waste are generated by septic systems every year. Properly run septic systems pose no problem, but those that are not properly built or maintained can be major polluters. Nearly 40 states have had groundwater contaminated by septic systems. Disease-carrying bacteria are the major problem caused by improperly built or maintained septic systems.

Mining pollutes waterways throughout the United States. Coal mines are the primary culprit, but uranium, copper, lead, zinc, iron, and other mines also contribute to the problem. Some 12,000 streams are estimated to be polluted by mine runoff.

Cities are a major source of water pollution. Municipal wastes from landfills often seep into the groundwater. Some municipal sewage treatment plants discharge wastes directly into rivers and lakes. And runoffs from heavy rains wash dirt, wastes, and pollutants from city streets into storm drains. From there they find their way into nearby rivers and lakes.

Agriculture is a major polluter of our rivers. Pesticides, fertilizers, hormones, and other agricultural chemicals leach into the ground and run off into rivers, streams, and lakes. More than 25 states report groundwater contaminated by pesticides. When many animals are herded together in feedlots, their wastes can also threaten water supplies.

And Then There Were None: Preserving Genetic Diversity

> Virtually all ecologists, and I include myself among them, would argue that every species extinction diminishes humanity.
>
> —E.O. Wilson, *Biodiversity*

THE MOST DRAMATIC mass extinction in history—that of the dinosaurs—seems like child's play compared to the one the world is undergoing today. Tens of thousands of species of animals, plants, and insects now vanish every year; noted biologist E.O. Wilson estimates that some 27,000 species become extinct every year in the rain forests alone. Other biologists approximate that from 10% to 20% of the estimated 10 million species of living things on our planet may disappear by the year 2020.

Some of those species have been hunted to extinction, but environmental destruction kills most. In some instances, pollution or pesticide is the culprit. In other instances, destroying an animal's food source will result in its demise. Introducing a foreign plant or animal into an established environment can cause similar destruction. Today, though, it is the widespread destruction of an entire ecosystem that often does the damage—most dramatically in the clearing of the rain forests.

Whatever its cause, each extinction decreases the earth's biodiversity. *Biodiversity* refers to the number of genetically diverse living things in our biosphere. In the crisis we face today, the problem is not merely that massive numbers of species are vanishing forever. It is also that the surviving plants and animals have a less rich genetic makeup than they had in the past. For example, farmers used to plant many more varieties of corn and wheat than they do today. Many of the older varieties have become extinct.

This massive loss of biodiversity has more than merely aesthetic effects. Each time a new plant or animal vanishes, we put ourselves in danger. Plants, for example, are a major source of new drugs. An estimated 30% of cancer-fighting medicines rely in one way or another upon plant extracts. Additionally, if we rely on only a few varieties of crops, there is a greater chance that those crops will be wiped out by disease or insects.

Sometimes, the way to save a species about to become extinct is clear-cut: Protect the environment in which that species lives. In other cases, though, we have to step in and use wildlife management and modern technology in order to save a species. That's what is currently being done to save the California condor, a massive, prehistoric vulture that once rode North American air currents and fed off the carcasses of such beasts as saber-toothed tigers and mastodons. If we can save the condor, and hundreds of thousands of other plant and animal species, it will prove that a bleak future is not, in fact, a foregone conclusion. And we will reap some very pragmatic benefits in the bargain, such as saving the environment that shelters the species.

Ways in Which Animal Species Become Extinct

Pollution, especially the widespread use of pesticides, is a major killer of animal species. Pesticides often do most of their harm to animals high up in the food chain, especially predators. That's because as you move up the food chain, pesticides can become increasingly concentrated—predators store pesticides in their fat instead of excreting them. The more pesticide-laden animals the predator eats, the greater the eventual accumulation in the predator, and the worse the effects. Peregrine falcons became endangered, for example, because DDT harmed their ability to breed. In a food chain, the top predator may contain 100 times more pesticide than an animal near the bottom.

Animals are frequently hunted for economic reasons—it is this type of hunting, more than sports hunting, that often puts species at risk. Some species, such as the anaconda and crocodile, are hunted for their skins. Others, such as the Bolson tortoise in Mexico, are hunted for their meat. And still others, such as elephants, are hunted for ivory.

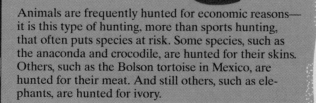

Some animals are deemed pests by humans, and so steps are consciously taken to eradicate them. Wolves, for example, have long been hunted by farmers, and subsequently have become increasingly rare.

When a foreign plant or animal, such as the cowbird shown on the right, is introduced into an ecosystem, often there is no local counterpart to keep it under control. The new population often soars and can displace a local plant or animal that formerly lived in the same environmental niche.

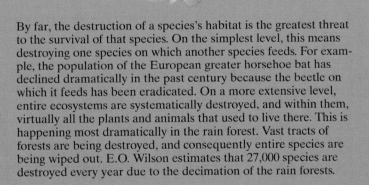

By far, the destruction of a species's habitat is the greatest threat to the survival of that species. On the simplest level, this means destroying one species on which another species feeds. For example, the population of the European greater horsehoe bat has declined dramatically in the past century because the beetle on which it feeds has been eradicated. On a more extensive level, entire ecosystems are systematically destroyed, and within them, virtually all the plants and animals that used to live there. This is happening most dramatically in the rain forest. Vast tracts of forests are being destroyed, and consequently entire species are being wiped out. E.O. Wilson estimates that 27,000 species are destroyed every year due to the decimation of the rain forests.

Estimated Annual Rate of Species Loss 1700–2000

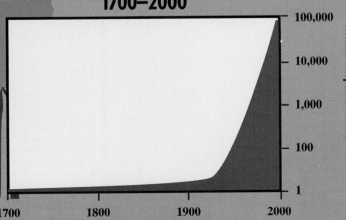

Source: Based on estimates in Norman Myers (ed.) *Gaia: An Atlas of Planet Management* (Garden City, NY Anchor Books, 1984), p.155

Saving the California Condor

6 The goal is to have a condor population that needs no human intervention in order to survive by the year 2010. To accomplish this, many more condors will have to be bred in captivity, and the ones released in the wild will have to survive and breed.

5 In January 1992, two California condors were released into the Sespe Condor Sanctuary, within the Los Padres National Forest in Southern California. Two Andean condors were also released to provide companionship; condors thrive when they have company. Since January 1992, an increasing number of condors have been released. Radio transmitters are attached to them so that they can be tracked. Calf carcasses are hauled up the mountains and placed where the condors can find them. Condors are scavengers; they eat the meat of animals already killed. They became endangered in the first place partly because they would eat carcasses of animals that hunters had shot and then die from lead poisoning from the hunters' bullets.

1 California condors are massive, prehistoric, vulture-like birds with 10-foot wingspans. They have existed since the last ice age, when they fed on the carcasses of saber-toothed tigers and mastodons. But by the 1980s, there were only 15 wild condors left and of those, only five pairs were breeding. So a plan went into effect to save them by restocking the wild population with birds that were bred in captivity. In the first phase of the plan, eggs were taken from condor nests in the wild and then hatched in zoos.

2 Between November 1984 and April 1985, 9 of the 15 condors remaining in the wild disappeared. Fearing that the entire condor population would suddenly be eradicated, biologists trapped the remaining birds and brought them to the San Diego Wild Animal Park and the Los Angeles Zoo for care and breeding. No condors were left in the wild.

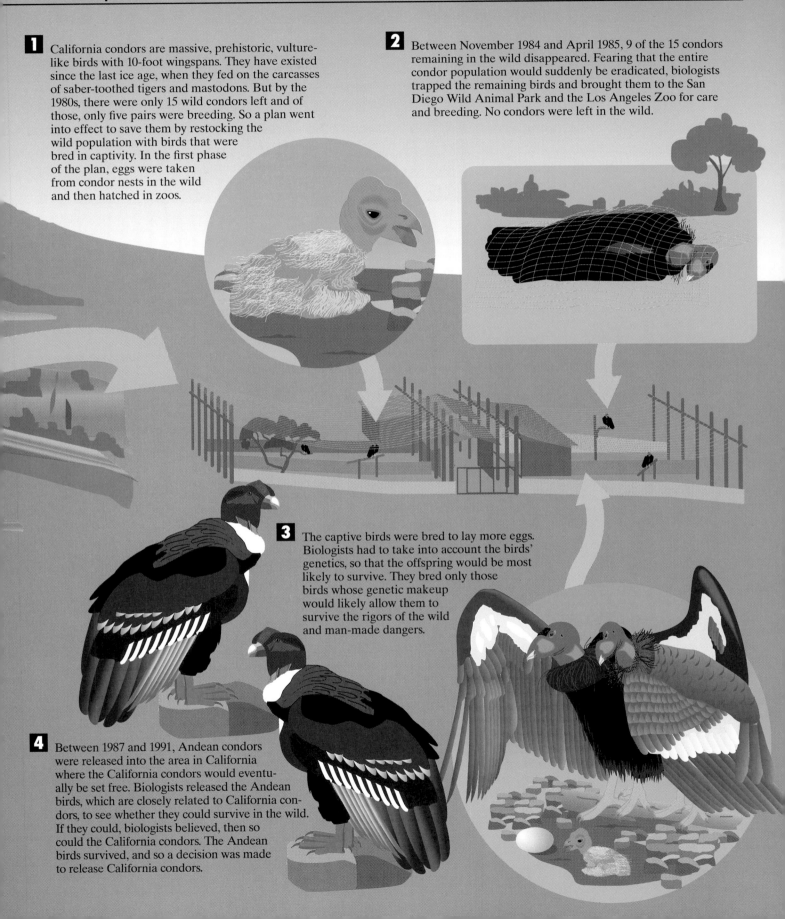

3 The captive birds were bred to lay more eggs. Biologists had to take into account the birds' genetics, so that the offspring would be most likely to survive. They bred only those birds whose genetic makeup would likely allow them to survive the rigors of the wild and man-made dangers.

4 Between 1987 and 1991, Andean condors were released into the area in California where the California condors would eventually be set free. Biologists released the Andean birds, which are closely related to California condors, to see whether they could survive in the wild. If they could, biologists believed, then so could the California condors. The Andean birds survived, and so a decision was made to release California condors.

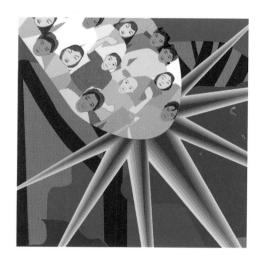

CHAPTER

6

The Population Bomb

THE EARTH IS not capable of efficiently supporting everyone on the planet…and it's only getting worse. That is the conclusion of many environmentalists when they look for the cause of our environmental woes. Overpopulation exacerbates just about every environmental problem on our planet, from air pollution to water degradation, from the creation of deserts to the fouling of our coasts.

There are approximately 5.6 billion people living on our planet today. The United Nations Population Division estimates that in all probability, there will be 10 billion by 2050, though the number could go as high as 12.5 billion by that time. If the earth is too taxed by its current population, consider what the world could be like then: a contaminated planet in which fertile land, fresh food, and clean air and water are difficult, if not impossible, to come by.

After a year-long study, a pair of Cornell University researchers concluded that the earth is only capable of sustaining a global population of 1 billion to 2 billion if we want to live in "relative prosperity" and if we do not want to destroy our environment. It is a sobering thought, considering the direction in which the population is headed.

Put simply, the human population may have exceeded the earth's carrying capacity, which is its ability to support us. There are too many of us, and we consume more resources than the sun and earth can create.

In general, population growth of the wealthiest and poorest nations, not of those in the middle, causes many of the problems. Though the richest nations tend to have the lowest rates of population growth, on average each person in a rich nation consumes far more resources than each person in a poor nation—up to 70 times more if you measure it by commercial energy use. Because of this, even small rates of population growth in rich nations lead to a great deal of environmental damage. The poorest nations tend to have the highest rates of population growth, leading them to overcultivate land and create deserts, destroy rain forests, and create massive urban pollution troubles.

There is a way to prevent the population bomb from detonating: We must institute population control. The birthrate must come down if we do not want to completely destroy the biosphere. This commitment requires political will and personal responsibility, two attributes we need to cultivate as a species.

How Overpopulation Harms the Environment

Increases in population require that more factories and power-generating plants be built. The airborne chemicals and gases that these industrial processes produce contribute to global warming, acid rain, and air pollution. Liquid and solid wastes pollute the land. Increased consumption of goods by the growing population creates a landfill crisis.

A growing population requires more clean, fresh water from the earth than the planet can possibly provide. Not only do we need water for drinking and bathing, but we also depend on it for farming and industry. As the population grows, less and less drinking water becomes available.

In order to feed a growing population, farmers in more developed countries use larger amounts of fertilizers, pesticides, and other agricultural chemicals. These pollute waterways and kill fish. Pesticides and chemicals work their way into the food chain, harming plants, animals, and ultimately, humans.

Population is growing fastest in parts of the world that can least afford to support more people: underdeveloped nations. In these countries, an increase in population forces many people to farm and live on *marginal land*—land that is most susceptible to environmental degradation. A steep wooded hillside is an example of marginal land. When trees are cleared from this type of hillside for farming, rains can easily wash away the topsoil, rendering it unsuitable for growing any kind of vegetation. Overcultivation and overgrazing of marginal lands leads to severe soil erosion and ultimately to *desertification*—the turning of once-fertile land into barren desert.

The pressure to feed a growing population causes forests to be cut and burned down so that they can be turned into farmland and grazing land. Additionally, a growing population needs more wood products, so even more forests are cut down. Rain forests are frequently the victims of these circumstances. Cutting down rain forests upsets a number of natural cycles. Forests can no longer filter pollution, nor can they take carbon dioxide out of the air. This can potentially lead to global warming. Tens of thousands of plant and animal species become extinct each year. Soil erosion and flooding can also result.

In many poor countries, the land on which people live becomes increasingly degraded as the rural population grows. People can no longer survive in the country so they move to cities. Overtaxed cities have no way of providing the proper services for a burgeoning, poverty-stricken population. Garbage dumps are unregulated, and water becomes polluted by human wastes, because city governments cannot afford to maintain proper sanitary services.

Growing Population, Shrinking Resources

	Circa 1990	2010	Total Change	Per Capita Change
	(million)		(percent)	
Population	5,290	7,030	+33	–
Fish Catch (tons)	85	102	+20	–10
Irrigated Land (hectares)	237	277	+17	–12
Cropland (hectares)	1,444	1,516	+5	–21
Rangeland and Pasture (hectares)	3,402	3,540	+4	–22
Forests (hectares)	3,413	3,165	–7	–30

Source: "State of the World 1994: A Worldwatch Institute Report on Progress Toward a Sustainable Society" (W.W. Norton, 1994) page 11

Population growth is exceeding the availability of renewable resources such as fisheries, farmland, forests, and rangeland. This chart details how the population will grow faster than renewable resources in the next 20 years. The first column shows the population and resources used in 1990; the second column shows estimates for 2010; the third column shows the change from 1990 to 2010; and the final column shows how much less of the resources will be available for each person in the world in 2010. (Note that one hectare equals 2.47 acres.)

HEALING THE LAND

CONTENTS

I N SOME CULTURES, the earth itself—the ground beneath our feet—is sacred. To desecrate it is to commit a sin. From this perspective, there is no doubt that we have disrespected the earth and are now suffering the consequences.

We are decimating our forests, destroying our farmland, polluting our cities, and poisoning land of every sort with garbage and hazardous wastes. In destroying our land, we also kill the animals and plants on it and disrupt the very functioning of the planet. When we chop down millions of acres of rain forests, for example, the damage is more than local in nature. Those forests help clean the air of pollution, regulate the climate, and maintain the proper balance between carbon dioxide and oxygen in our atmosphere. Their absence disrupts the earth's balance, and the consequences range from local flooding to global warming.

Rain forests are, biologically speaking, among the richest places on earth. When rain forests are destroyed, so are tens of thousands of unique plants and animals. Forest-dwelling plants and animals may seem of no use to us in industrialized societies, but in fact, many of our lives depend upon them. Many cancer-fighting and other helpful drugs are first discovered in plants found only in the rain forests. And it's not only drugs that are found there: Many food crops now grown throughout the world originated in rain forests and were later domesticated for widespread use. The rain forest is a kind of genetic warehouse that we can turn to when needed—but what happens after it's been destroyed?

It is important to keep in mind that we are the ones who suffer the ultimate injury when we harm the land. When we overuse pesticides, not only do birds and fish suffer, but humans do also. Pesticides kill thousands of people a year—primarily agricultural workers—by poisoning them. Pesticide residues in our foods may kill people by causing cancers. The same holds true for dumping hazardous wastes. This practice scars the earth and causes human casualties because of the deleterious health effects.

Population growth also has an adverse impact on the earth's land. As the population grows, usable earth becomes rarer and more precious. Not only is there less land to go around as there are more of us, but population pressures also destroy the usable land. For example, pressures to feed growing populations force those in third-world countries to farm land that cannot easily sustain agriculture, which turns those lands into deserts. Similarly, chopping down forests to obtain firewood also turns land into desert. In addition, we also use more and more land as sites for storing garbage. Even farming, which may seem like one of the best uses for land, extracts its environmental toll: Agricultural chemicals such as fertilizers and pesticides pollute the land and water.

In all of this, there is at least some good news: While there are ways in which we have exploited the land, we are also smart enough to start saving it. It is no accident that environmental awareness is running high in the industrialized countries of the world—places where the land has been severely and visibly damaged. Because of this, industrialized nations have been passing environmental laws to mitigate what has been done.

In some developing countries, such as China, environmental matters have taken a back seat to economic priorities. In many cases, these countries are repeating mistakes that the developed countries have already made. However, in other developing countries, there has been a recognition that economic development and environmental protection can go hand in hand. In Indonesia, for example, natural pest-control methods have replaced the widespread use of pesticides in rice growing. The result is not only a cleaner environment, but also an economic boon for farmers: Since they no longer spray massive amounts of pesticides, their farming costs are lower and they are in better financial shape.

In this section, we'll look at how we have destroyed the land and how we are healing it. Chapter 7 discusses the controversy surrounding the spotted owl and the ancient forests of the Pacific Northwest. This issue has become a symbol of how economic pressures clash with environmental concerns. Chapter 8 covers the remarkable ecology of tropical rain forests and how they're being destroyed, to the entire world's detriment. Chapter 9 examines how modern agriculture can cause severe environmental damage. You'll also hear some good news in this chapter about how farming can be environmentally friendly.

Chapter 10 details how we are destroying fertile land and turning it into desert. Chapter 11 focuses on one of the successes of the environmental movement: recycling. You'll see how paper and even entire automobiles are recycled, and you'll learn about an environmentally friendly landfill. Finally, in Chapter 12, you'll see how hazardous waste sites can be cleaned up, in many cases by using bacteria to literally eat the waste.

In some ways, the outlook for our environment is bleak, but in other ways, there are more than a few rays of hope. Technology and industry are often part of the answer, even though they have helped to create many environmental problems. They have also created new techniques for healing the land. The real questions now are: Will we be smart enough to develop those techniques and use them wisely? And are we willing to change the way we use the land so that we do not scar it in the first place?

CHAPTER 7

Old-Growth Forests and Spotted Owls

THERE ARE PROBABLY no greater symbols of our ambivalence toward the environment than the humble 16-inch-tall spotted owl and the majestic Douglas fir. Together, these two tell a story of past injustices toward the environment, and of current economic forces clashing with nature.

Both live in old-growth forests in the Pacific Northwest. Old-growth trees, such as the massive Douglas firs that populate the Northwest, are among nature's marvels. Some of them have been alive for more than 1,000 years and tower more than 300 feet high. These forests provide more than aesthetic delight—they also clean the air of pollutants, remove carbon dioxide from and add oxygen to the atmosphere, prevent soil erosion and flooding, and gather water for the land below.

Logging has taken its toll on the old-growth forests that once covered much of the Northwest. The practice of clear-cutting is often the culprit. *Clear-cutting* is a logging technique that cuts a swath through the forest; instead of cutting some trees and leaving others in an area, loggers fell all the trees in that area, leaving a naked scar in the forest. In addition to killing the forest in that one area, clear-cutting endangers other sections of the forest. A mild bird called the spotted owl is also a victim of clear-cutting. This owl has become endangered because it can only live in old-growth forests. Logging has been halted in parts of the Northwest in order to protect this increasingly rare bird. Unfortunately, this threatens the logging industry, and has been a great source of conflict between environmentalists and loggers.

The entire ecosystem of the forest is of equal importance to the environmentalists. The spotted owl is significant because it is an *indicator species*. This means that if the spotted owl population cannot maintain a *critical mass* (the minimum animal population necessary to sustain a species indefinitely), the overall health of the forest may be in jeopardy. In other words, if the spotted owl is in danger, then so is the entire forest. So protecting the spotted owl helps protect the entire forest.

There are those who believe that New Forestry may be the solution to protecting the owls and forests, as well as aiding loggers, a way of managing forests that prevents the forest from irreparable harm. Others believe that the answer is in using recycled alternatives to wood products and decreasing the use of wood products. The solution probably involves implementing a combination of these proposals. Only then will the owl and the logger be able to live in harmony within old-growth forests.

How Old-Growth Forests and Spotted Owls Coexist

Old-growth forests, also known as ancient forests, have been untouched for centuries and are filled with old, massive trees such as Douglas firs that may grow to over 300 feet high. The very top layer of the greenery is called a canopy and it serves several purposes. It collects moisture for the forest from fog and passing clouds. It provides shelter for the plants and animals below from the cold and snow in winter and from the heat in summer.

The spotted owl is a predator that feeds on small mammals such as squirrels. By controlling the population of squirrels and other animals that feed on truffles, the owls ensure that these fungi will not be completely eaten, which would endanger the forest.

Spotted owls do not build their own homes, but nest in broken treetops and in cavities in large, old trees. The owls are an integral part of the old-growth forests' ecosystem and have adapted to it in many ways. In fact, they have adapted to it so well that they are considered an indicator species. This means that if they are endangered, the old-growth forest as a whole is endangered as well.

The forest canopy filters the light that enters the forest, inhibiting the growth of too many trees. The result is that trees are farther away from one another than in younger forests. This spacing of trees provides enough flying room so that airborne predators such as the spotted owl can thrive. The canopy allows enough sunlight for some younger trees to grow, and these younger trees form canopies below the top canopy within the forest.

A remarkable ecosystem can be found at the very bottom of the forest. Beneath the soil, *mycorrhizal* fungi wrap themselves tightly around the roots of trees. These fungi help the trees by absorbing minerals and water from the soil and making them available to the tree through its roots. In return, the fungi get nutrition from the tree's roots.

Fallen trees and decaying plants on the forest floor provide homes for many insects, lizards, rodents such as mice and squirrels, and other small animals. Squirrels, mice, and other animals feed on truffles, which are the fruit of some of the mycorrhizal fungi wrapped around the trees' roots. These animals then excrete spores from the truffles throughout the forest. From these spores, new truffles grow, and so are spread throughout the forests.

How Clear-Cutting Destroys Old-Growth Forests

Old-growth trees act as massive water gatherers by trapping moisture from fog and passing clouds and passing it to the forest below. When the trees are cut and can no longer gather moisture, nearby reservoirs may run low because much less water runs into them from forest streams. The trees also act as air purifiers by absorbing pollution from the air. When they are cut down, they can no longer clean the air.

Forests at the edge of the clear-cut also suffer damage. Trees there have to contend with winds, and they may be blown down. Clear-cutting can also kill fungi living in the soil that are vitally important to an old-growth forest's health. When these fungi are gone from the soil, trees no longer regenerate and also grow more slowly.

Some animals and insects will refuse to cross a clear-cut area. Spotted owls, for instance, often do not cross because when they do they are exposed to a larger owl predator. This leads to the creation of "islands" of wildlife in which the population may not be large enough to breed. In order to maintain a self-sustaining population, there needs to be a critical mass of wildlife in any given area. A critical mass refers to the minimum size of an animal population that is required for sustaining the population indefinitely.

Clear-cutting refers to a method of harvesting trees in which large swaths of forest are cut down at once. All the vegetation in that area is destroyed, while the forest is left untouched on each side of the clear-cut. In some instances, rotted fallen trees, ground vegetation, tree stumps, and other vegetation are cleared by *slash burning*—burning everything in the cut area after the trees have been harvested. The resulting smoke pollutes the air not only in the forest but in cities as well. Massive amounts of carbon dioxide (CO_2) are released from these fires and may contribute to global warming. One estimate holds that it takes 200 years for newly planted trees to reclaim from the atmosphere the CO_2 released when an ancient forest is cut.

With no tree roots or other vegetation to protect the soil in a clear-cut, the soil is washed away, making it difficult for other things to grow there. Rain causes landslides and mudslides and washes the soil into nearby streams.

Mudslides caused by erosion can severely damage streams. In one case, mudslides wiped out a salmon-rearing habitat so badly that it is estimated the habitat won't recover for 150 years. Temperatures in the streams rise because they are no longer shaded by the canopy of forest. This harms and even kills fish and insects in the stream.

CHAPTER 8

Nature's Eden: Tropical Rain Forests

ENCIRCLING THE GLOBE in a worldwide band to the north and south of the equator, one of the most remarkable ecosystems imaginable can be found—the tropical rain forest. Fed by year-round equatorial warmth and frequent rains, rain forests are home to an almost unimaginable variety of every kind of life, from microorganisms to insects, plants, and animals.

Tropical rain forests are so fecund that while they only make up about 7% of the land on the earth, they are home to an estimated 50% to 90% of all living species. Approximately half of all the growing wood on earth can be found within them.

Much of this life never touches the ground. The top of a tropical rain forest is called the canopy. A canopy is made up of the leaves of enormous trees, as well as many plants, flowers, and fruits. *Epiphytes*, plants that live on other plants instead of on the ground, also live here, and are often remarkable mini-ecosystems unto themselves. Hundreds of thousands of species of animals and birds live within the canopy, from moths, caterpillars, butterflies, and other insects, all the way up to tree-living monkeys, parrots, eagles, and other birds.

The forests' largest trees, called emergents, pierce through the top of the canopy. And at the very bottom of the forest are smaller plants, insects, animals such as wild boars and leopards, and microorganisms that help recycle dead plant and animal matter into nutrients to feed the trees.

Though you may never see a tropical rain forest except on a poster or nature television show, their existence is vital to your life. Because they hold most of the world's species, they are a vast genetic resource for humankind. Many modern medicines owe their existence to a plant or an animal originally found in the rain forest. Many foods that we eat originated there as well. When a crop is endangered by a pest or blight, agricultural scientists often turn to the rain forest to see what kind of related plant in that region can be crossbred with the endangered one so that the resulting crop will be pest-resistant.

Tropical rain forests serve even more diverse ecological purposes. The enormous amount of plant matter in them takes in carbon dioxide during photosynthesis and releases oxygen. This helps to rid us of a greenhouse gas, carbon dioxide, that can help make the planet too warm. With less forest to remove carbon dioxide, the carbon dioxide level rises—contributing to global warming.

Tropical rain forests also do much to maintain regional water cycles and to prevent soil erosion—and when the forests are cut down there can be catastrophic consequences. Forests normally hold water in soil after heavy rains and during the rainy season; in dry seasons that water is slowly released back into streams so that the streams don't dry up. This delicate balancing act averts both flooding and drought.

Rain forests everywhere are under attack. They are being burned down to clear the land for farming and grazing, even though their soil is suitable for neither. They are being chopped down for firewood and to feed the developed world's insatiable need for wood products. They are vanishing at the rate of 1½ acres every second.

There is some hope, though. The world is finally awakening to how vital tropical rain forests are to all of humankind's health, and treaties have been signed to try to save them. Even industries have recognized that these forests are not an endless resource, and so must be cared for. For example, Merck & Company, a pharmaceutical business, signed a $1 million contract with an institute for biodiversity in the tropics. Merck will receive samples of tropical plants and leaves from the institute in order to investigate whether any are medicinally important.

Although we have destroyed much of the rain forest, there is still time to save the rest.

The Ecology of Rain Forests

Plant and animal life in rain forests is richest at the very top of the forest. Life is incredibly varied here; there are thousands of species of plants, animals, amphibians, birds, and insects. Animals often spend their entire lives up here without ever touching the ground.

Many complex food chains are within the canopy. They are all based on the forest's rich plant life, including fruits, nuts, and seeds, as well as leaves. Animals such as monkeys, parrots, fruit bats, and sloths live off the plants. Insects such as caterpillars feed on the leaves, and in turn are eaten by frogs and other insect-eaters. And plant-eaters and insect-eaters are in turn consumed by predators, such as eagles.

Fungi, beetles, earthworms, microscopic bacteria, and termites that teem at the bottom of the forest floor feed on dead wood, fallen leaves, and dead plants and animals. These organisms break down dead plant and animal matter into nutrients that then feed the forest's trees and plants. The soil is rich with these recyclers: A fraction of a cubic inch of rain forest soil can contain billions of bacteria and yards of fungal threads. Rain forest soil itself is actually poor in nutrients, but recyclers break down dead plants and animals into their nutrients with incredible speed—a tree may be recycled in a matter of weeks, instead of months, as is the case in forests in more temperate climates.

Within the canopy's large ecosystem are many small, intricate ecosystems. One of the more interesting ecosystems centers around the epiphytic plants that live on top of other plants. Water is trapped in the flume-shaped centers of the plants. Within that small puddle, tree frogs lay their eggs, tadpoles grow, and the larvae of insects live. Animals come to drink, and are eaten by snakes who lie in wait for them. Some small animals who come to drink drown in the water, and the nutrients from their decomposing bodies feed the plants.

The rain forest soil is thin, and nutrients are found only in the very top layer. Because of this, trees put down extremely shallow roots—generally less than 18 inches deep. In order to hold up the massive trees, wide-ranging *buttress roots* often grow up the first 15 to 20 feet of the trunk.

There is very little undergrowth in a tropical forest because the canopy above lets little light in, and plants cannot grow without sunlight. However, some shrubs and trees do manage to grow, and they create a second canopy below the topmost one. While most animals live on the canopy above, there is also animal life below. Some animals, such as anteaters, live off insects. Others, such as deer and monkeys, live off plants and fruits. And there are also predators, such as leopards.

How Rain Forests Are Destroyed

Deforestation exacts a tremendous toll on the regional and global environment. One major effect is the possible hastening of global warming. When vast tracts of forest are cut down, huge amounts of greenhouse gases such as carbon dioxide are released into the atmosphere. These gases trap heat on the earth's surface.

Slash-and-burn farming traditionally has been used in tropical rain forests. On a small scale, it is not overly damaging to rain forests, but when massive areas of vegetation are slashed, burned, and then farmed, the results are catastrophic. Rain forest soils are typically nutrient-poor, so the ashes from the fire provide much-needed soil nutrition. In traditional slash-and-burn farming, after a few years when the nutrients are gone, a new area is burned and the previous area left fallow, often for decades, to recover nutrients. In more modern times, these nutrient-depleted areas are given over to grazing animals, or else are farmed too soon, leading to massive soil erosion. Slash-and-burn farming has caused some 35% of deforestation of tropical rain forests in Latin America, almost 50% in Asia, and 70% in Africa.

Rain forests are cut down not only to clear the way for agriculture, but also for the wood in them. Low-cost energy is hard to find in developing countries where tropical rain forests are often found, so the forests are cut down for firewood. Additionally, tropical woods such as mahogany and teak are in great demand in more developed parts of the world, so trees are cut for their timber value. A smaller amount of rain forest is cut down to make way for plantations of tropical trees such as rubber and eucalyptus.

Tropical rain forests take up an estimated 7% of the earth's surface, yet they harbor up to 90% of all plant and animal species. These species are being lost at an alarming rate every year—with potentially dire consequences. Many modern medicines were first discovered as plants or as chemicals in animals in the tropics, so we are harming our own health by destroying potentially beneficial wildlife. Additionally, there is a vast gene pool of diverse plants from which we can draw to improve agricultural practices. For example, when a deadly virus was destroying the barley crop in California, and disease was decimating the sugar cane crop in Louisiana, wild variants of those crops from rain forests were crossbred with domesticated ones—and new, disease-resistant plants were developed.

When forests are cut down, there are no roots to hold the soil or the water, so during heavy rains, flooding occurs. During these rains, soil is eroded into waterways, which become silted up. During the dry season, no water is available for plants or animals to use because waterways have been filled up with silt.

Across the world, tropical rain forests are home to indigenous people who have adapted to them and developed their own unique cultures. When forests are cut down, these traditional ways of life cannot be maintained because the forest resources are no longer available, leading to the destruction of the tribes themselves. This hurts those in the developed world as well as the indigenous people, because the forest-dwellers have a great deal of knowledge about the medicinal uses of plants that could lead to medical breakthroughs.

53

Our Breadbasket

OUR GROWING POPULATION is due in part to modern farming techniques. Nothing is more essential to the survival of the human species than farming. The yield of food per acre has skyrocketed in the twentieth century, owing to the "green revolution." The green revolution involves the use of modern machinery and an arsenal of technology, including chemicals such as fertilizers and pesticides to increase food output. The green revolution has been of particular help to third-world countries, since it allows a relatively small number of farmers to feed a large population.

But this bounty has come at a cost: Chemical fertilizers do damage when they are washed into waterways, lakes, and underground aquifers. They also poison water supplies and kill off aquatic life. In addition, chemical fertilizers destroy the soil's natural balance. This makes the soil vulnerable to erosion, leaves it lacking in nutrients, and starts a vicious cycle in which more fertilizer must be used to make up for soil depletion. And chemical pesticides in particular do an enormous amount of environmental harm. They kill fish, birds, and other wildlife, and can devastate entire species and ecosystems.

A study of Lake Michigan examined the effects of pesticides that worked their way through the food chain. The study found the lake contained a concentration of .014 parts per million of pesticides in the bottom mud; .44 parts per million in shrimp, which are fairly low on the food chain; 5.6 parts per million in whitefish, which are higher up the food chain; and 98.9 parts per million in herring gulls, which are at the top of the food chain—approximately 7,000 times the concentration found in bottom mud.

Pesticide poisonings didn't diminish when the infamous DDT was banned from use in the United States in 1972; pesticides killed at least 1 million fish in Southern Louisiana during the 1991 growing season. Pesticides poison an estimated 1 million people a year, with up to 20,000 deaths worldwide; most of the effects are felt by those applying the pesticides. And pesticides kill not only insect pests, but also the predators that feed on them, which means that an ever-increasing amount of pesticides will be needed to control the pest population.

So modern agriculture yields a harvest of more than fruits, vegetables and meats—it also produces environmental devastation. Farmland and grazing land may be beautiful to look at, but agricultural practices can also contribute to everything from the mass killing of fish and birds, to the pollution of ground water, the creation of deserts, and the production of some human cancers.

For example, the Midwest has some of the most fertile soil in the world. However, plowing the land every spring dries it out, making it vulnerable to being washed into rivers by heavy rains or blown away by the wind. Heavy farm machinery compacts the soil so water cannot penetrate through it to feed plants. Modern agricultural practices, such as plowing the fields with heavy equipment, have eroded the farm soil itself. These factors clearly diminish the amount of arable farmland available for agriculture.

Increasingly, farmers recognize the problem—and they see that good environmental practices also often mean higher profits for them. For example, in the highly mechanized U.S. farm industry, a full quarter of all farmland is no longer subject to the environmentally damaging process of using heavy machinery to plow each spring. Farmers instead leave the stubble and decomposing plant matter from the previous year's planting, and scratch in new seeds. This means the soil doesn't dry out and erode, and it also recycles vital nutrients in the decaying matter. This practice saves farmers an estimated $25 per acre in costs. The U.S. Soil Conservation Service estimates that farmers of 80% of all American farmland will employ this technique by the end of the century.

More and more, farmers across the world are also rotating crops, being more careful in their use of water, and using manure and other organic fertilizers instead of chemical ones. The practices of growing the same crops on the soil year after year and using chemical fertilizers destroy the organic matter in the soil, making it vulnerable to erosion. All in all, farmers have discovered that feeding the world and caring for the environment need not conflict.

How Farming and Pesticides Harm the Environment

1 Around the world, farming is seriously eroding the soil, and pesticides are polluting the water supply. It is estimated that soil in the United States is being lost at 16 times the rate at which it is being formed. Soil is not just dirt; it is a finely balanced ecosystem that has taken tens of thousands, and in some cases millions, of years to form. Soil contains minerals, nutrients, organic matter, and living microorganisms, which together provide a perfect environment for growing food. According to the Natural Resources Defense Council, an estimated 845 million pounds of pesticides are applied to U.S. farmland every year. The chemicals do more than kill insect pests; they also cause a significant amount of environmental damage. Pesticides applied to crops are washed by the rain into rivers and lakes. From there they work their way up through the food chain, doing damage along the way.

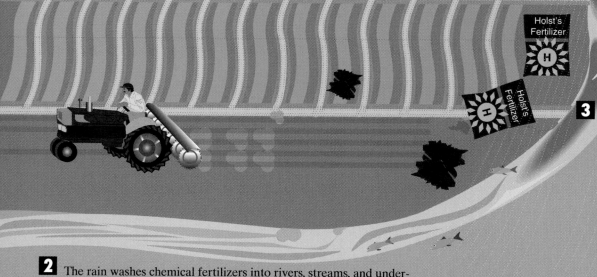

Holst's Fertilizer
H

Holst's Fertilizer
H

3 Pesticides and herbicides used in farming are toxic not only to pests, but also to other plants and animals, including people. These chemicals wash into rivers, lakes, and streams, and they leach into the water supply. They also make their way into the food chain and kill many animals, often with devastating efficiency. Pesticide poisoning of farm workers and other people is commonplace, particularly in impoverished countries.

2 The rain washes chemical fertilizers into rivers, streams, and underground water supplies. The phosphates and nitrogen in the fertilizers cause lakes to *eutrophy*, or lead to the growth of certain bacteria that use up all the oxygen in the lake. This leaves no oxygen for animal and plant life, and so water life is killed. Fertilizers washed into water supplies render them toxic and undrinkable. Byproducts of fertilizers, such as nitrous oxide, pollute the air and help cause global warming due to the greenhouse effect.

10 Agriculture affects water supplies in a number of ways. Lakes, reservoirs, and streams can be filled with silt when soil washes off farmland. Manure from farm animals washes into water supplies and pollutes them. The overuse of water for agriculture has led to the depletion of groundwater and aquifers, leading to water shortages. One estimate holds that more than half of all the water used in the United States goes toward growing feed for livestock.

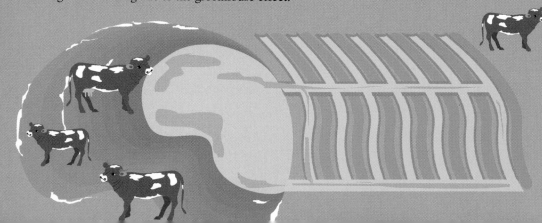

6 Pesticide-contaminated insects are eaten by animals, especially birds, who can be harmed or killed by pesticides. In one midwestern city, for example, DDT was sprayed on elm trees to fight off insect pests. DDT-resistant worms ate the elm leaves. Robins ate the worms, and the robin population declined.

7 Pesticides kill not only pests, but also pollinating bees, and other insects that feed on those pests—leading to the possibility that pest populations will explode once their natural predators are eliminated.

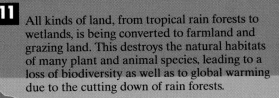

11 All kinds of land, from tropical rain forests to wetlands, is being converted to farmland and grazing land. This destroys the natural habitats of many plant and animal species, leading to a loss of biodiversity as well as to global warming due to the cutting down of rain forests.

8 Farm workers are poisoned when pesticides are sprayed on them, or when they work in pesticide-laced fields. A 1989 World Health Organization and United Nations Environmental Programme report estimated that 1 million people are poisoned by pesticides each year worldwide, and that there are about 20,000 deaths. That doesn't take into account the potential long-term health dangers posed by pesticides, such as increased rates of cancer. A recent study found that children of farm workers exposed to pesticides are more likely to be born with biliary atresia, a rare liver disorder.

5 Pesticides wash through the soil into underground aquifers, and also make their way into aquifers from rivers and streams that have been contaminated with pesticides. Well water comes from aquifers, so people who use the well water drink pesticide-laced water. A 1990 Environmental Protection Agency report found that 10% of the wells tested contained pesticides.

9 Pesticides often cannot be washed off fruits and vegetables; residues are commonly found in food. One estimate holds that 40% of supermarket foods are contaminated with pesticides. Long-range health effects of this kind of pesticide exposure have not yet been determined, although it has been implicated in a variety of cancers. Additionally, improper handling of foods and pesticides can lead to extremely high levels of pesticides in foods. In 1994 in China, more than 200 students were poisoned by pesticides when they ate pesticide-laced vegetables in their school cafeteria.

4 Microscopic plants and animals in the water ingest pesticides and are in turn eaten by small fish. If the pesticides are the type stored in fat instead of excreted, they become concentrated in the fish. Larger fish then eat smaller fish, and the larger fish store increasing amounts of pesticides. Fish near the top of the food chain ingest the highest concentration of pesticides and can be killed by them. Birds that feed on fish contain even higher concentrations, and are frequently killed as well.

Environment-Friendly Farming

1 Farming need not wreak environmental havoc to produce high yields of crops or profits for farmers. In fact, *sustainable agriculture* can be even more profitable than farming that harms the environment, because use of expensive pesticides and fertilizer is minimized. This agricultural method takes into account the impact of farming on the environment.

2 In order to prevent erosion, farmers can do away with the old practice of plowing their fields every spring in order to plant crops. Instead, they leave the residue and stubble from last year's crop on the soil, and scratch seeds through the decomposing plant matter. This helps the soil retain moisture and nutrients, and it prevents erosion. This *conservation tillage* saves farmers money as well: Farmers report saving $25 per acre in costs because they don't have to plow before planting.

3 Instead of using chemical fertilizers that are expensive and dangerous to the environment, farmers can use animal manure and decomposing plant matter to fertilize their fields. This helps build the soil so that it is richer in nutrients, and it does away with the pollution caused by chemical fertilizers. This practice also prevents damage to waterways and aquifers by animal wastes that would otherwise wash into them.

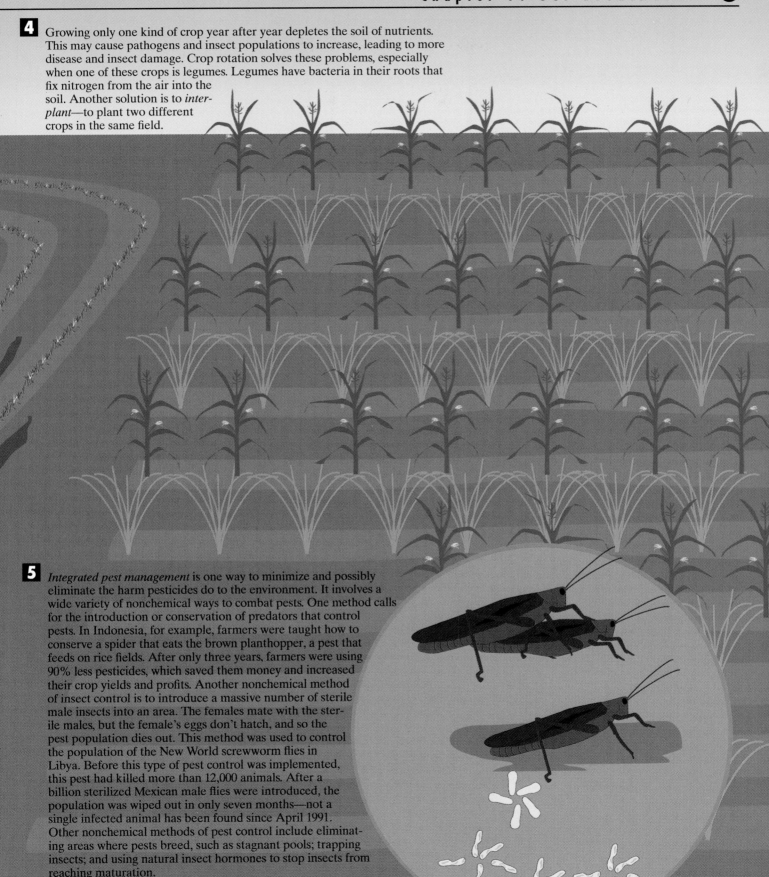

4 Growing only one kind of crop year after year depletes the soil of nutrients. This may cause pathogens and insect populations to increase, leading to more disease and insect damage. Crop rotation solves these problems, especially when one of these crops is legumes. Legumes have bacteria in their roots that fix nitrogen from the air into the soil. Another solution is to *interplant*—to plant two different crops in the same field.

5 *Integrated pest management* is one way to minimize and possibly eliminate the harm pesticides do to the environment. It involves a wide variety of nonchemical ways to combat pests. One method calls for the introduction or conservation of predators that control pests. In Indonesia, for example, farmers were taught how to conserve a spider that eats the brown planthopper, a pest that feeds on rice fields. After only three years, farmers were using 90% less pesticides, which saved them money and increased their crop yields and profits. Another nonchemical method of insect control is to introduce a massive number of sterile male insects into an area. The females mate with the sterile males, but the female's eggs don't hatch, and so the pest population dies out. This method was used to control the population of the New World screwworm flies in Libya. Before this type of pest control was implemented, this pest had killed more than 12,000 animals. After a billion sterilized Mexican male flies were introduced, the population was wiped out in only seven months—not a single infected animal has been found since April 1991. Other nonchemical methods of pest control include eliminating areas where pests breed, such as stagnant pools; trapping insects; and using natural insect hormones to stop insects from reaching maturation.

CHAPTER 10

How Humankind Creates Deserts

THE SCENES ARE horrifying: people starving to death in widespread famines; desert where there was once fruitful land; soil blowing away in the wind. The extended drought that turned African grazing land and farmland into barren desert is often considered an act of nature. Africa is not the only continent that has been victimized by desert encroachment. On average, 40 square miles of our earth becomes desert every single day, and there is no end in sight. We can't chalk all this up to Mother Nature.

Humankind is the primary creator of deserts today. We are relentlessly turning land into infertile wasteland that supports few living things. This process is called *desertification,* and the resulting deserts are different than those that occur naturally. Natural deserts have a stark beauty, and they support a surprisingly complex and rich variety of plants and animals. The human-created deserts are anything but beautiful. And because they are less mature than natural deserts, they lack diverse plants and animals.

Human-made deserts are generally created on dry land that is found on the edge of existing desert. This dry land is vulnerable to environmental degradation. In 1984, the United Nations estimated that over one-third of the earth's ice-free land, an area that supports more than 1 billion people, had the potential for turning into desert. The U.N. also reported that a full three-quarters of that land had already showed signs of damage.

Human population pressures are primarily to blame for this predicament. Land that cannot really support agriculture or grazing is being exploited in order to feed a growing population; this is especially true in developing nations. The land is not able to bear this burden for long. The soil becomes severely malnourished, or the grasses are excessively grazed. As a result, the soil erodes and is blown away by wind and washed away by water. When the rains do come, there is no soil to hold in the water, so flooding occurs. Deforestation—the widespread use of trees for fuel—is another byproduct of overpopulation and also causes desertification.

Undeniably, drought is a major cause of desertification. But there are some environmentalists who believe that humankind has to bear some of the blame for this as well. They say that the global warming we create leads to less rainfall, which helps create deserts.

There are, however, solutions to the problem. Land that has been turned into desert can be reclaimed through proper irrigation and reforestation. Restraints on human population growth can reduce our role in the creation of deserts. Smarter farming and grazing techniques can ensure that vulnerable land does not turn into desert. What we have done we can undo—and we can make sure that in future years millions of people are not subjected to a human-created catastrophe masquerading as an act of nature.

How We Create Deserts

Vast deserts are being created on almost every continent—and not by the work of nature, but by the actions of humankind. The creation of these deserts from once-productive land leads to widespread famine and disease that kill millions of people.

When trees and other woody plants are chopped down for firewood, topsoil is lost to erosion, and desertification can result.

The overgrazing of land is one major cause of desertification. When animals such as cattle and sheep graze too much on dry grasslands, they eat more vegetation than the land can grow back. They also compact the soil so that water cannot penetrate it, preventing plants from being nourished. Both of these factors lead to the loss of vegetation. With no roots to hold the soil, wind blows it away and rain washes it off. Plants can no longer grow under these conditions.

Overfarming also causes desertification. When crops are grown on soil that is not rich in nutrients, the land needs time between plantings to recuperate and build up nutrients. When instead the land is cultivated and not allowed to lie fallow, it eventually loses its ability to grow any vegetation at all—leading to erosion by wind and rain.

Poor irrigation techniques can cause desertification. When plants are irrigated too heavily without proper drainage, their roots become waterlogged and they die. When this kind of poor irrigation is combined with the use of chemical fertilizers, salt deposits form in the soil and on the plants' roots and leaves, which kills the plants. Similarly, irrigation water may contain alkaline chemicals, which also kill plants.

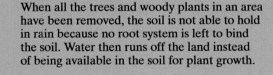

When all the trees and woody plants in an area have been removed, the soil is not able to hold in rain because no root system is left to bind the soil. Water then runs off the land instead of being available in the soil for plant growth.

There are some who believe that global warming has helped create deserts across the world because when the earth warms, less rain falls. This leads to droughts and the creation of deserts.

Recycling and the Landfill Crisis

WE ARE DROWNING in garbage and solid waste. Tons and tons and tons of it—about 10 billion metric tons each and every year in the United States. This waste is a combination of household garbage (each person in the United States throws away 3.5 pounds of waste per day) and solid waste created by industry. To call us a throwaway society is an understatement.

To make matters worse, there are fewer and fewer places in which garbage can be disposed of. There were some 20,000 landfills in operation in the United States in 1978; by 1993 that number had shrunk to an estimated 4,000. It is no surprise, then, that barges sent from the United States to find a country where refuse can be dumped discover that no one else wants their cargoes either, and that they are often forced to return to port with their cargoes intact.

When garbage is disposed of in landfills, it can create serious problems for the surrounding region. *Leachate*, a liquid produced in landfills, can poison the surrounding water supplies and soil. Methane gas, also created in landfills, can build up and explode when ignited by a spark.

But the garbage problem in our society runs deeper than the disposal of wastes. Energy and raw materials are required to produce everything we discard heedlessly. When this energy and these raw materials are used in the manufacturing process, air pollution, water pollution, and other environmental destruction results. If we used more of what we threw away, not only would our landfill crisis be eased, but so would many other environmental problems.

There are several answers to the predicament. One is for industries to be more efficient when they manufacture products so that they produce less waste and use fewer resources. Another is to recycle and reuse. Paper, cardboard, plastic, glass, cans, yard wastes, and even entire automobiles can be recycled and used again. And our landfills and incinerators can be made safer so that they do not damage the environment.

Recycling is one area in which every person can have an immediate impact. Almost every town and city in the country has either a voluntary or mandatory recycling program in place. Collect your cans, plastic, glass, and paper and bring it to a recycling center. Or, if you're lucky enough, leave it curbside for your city or town to pick up. When you recycle, not only will you justifiably feel that you've done a good deed—you'll also ensure yourself a cleaner, safer world.

How Paper Is Recycled

Paper can be recycled in many different ways and into many different products. For example, used computer paper or stationery often goes toward making new computer paper and stationery. One of the most common uses for recycled paper is in creating chipboard or boxboard—the kind of material used in packaging products such as cereal boxes.

2 The paper is loaded onto conveyer belts and dropped into huge vats of warm water called depulpers. These depulpers can hold approximately 4 tons of material. The paper sits in the vats for approximately 45 minutes, and turns into a mush the consistency of oatmeal. A powerful magnet in the vat attracts metal objects such as paper clips and staples, and these are disposed of.

1 Typically, boxboard is made of eight layers of recycled papers, although it can be made of six or fewer layers. The two outer layers, called liner layers, need to be of a higher quality than the inner layers because they may be printed upon, and because consumers see them. Used paper material that will be recycled for the six inner layers—such as phone books, catalogs, and junk mail—is dumped outside the paper mill. The higher-quality material for the outer layers—such as newspaper and cardboard—is brought in bales into the mill.

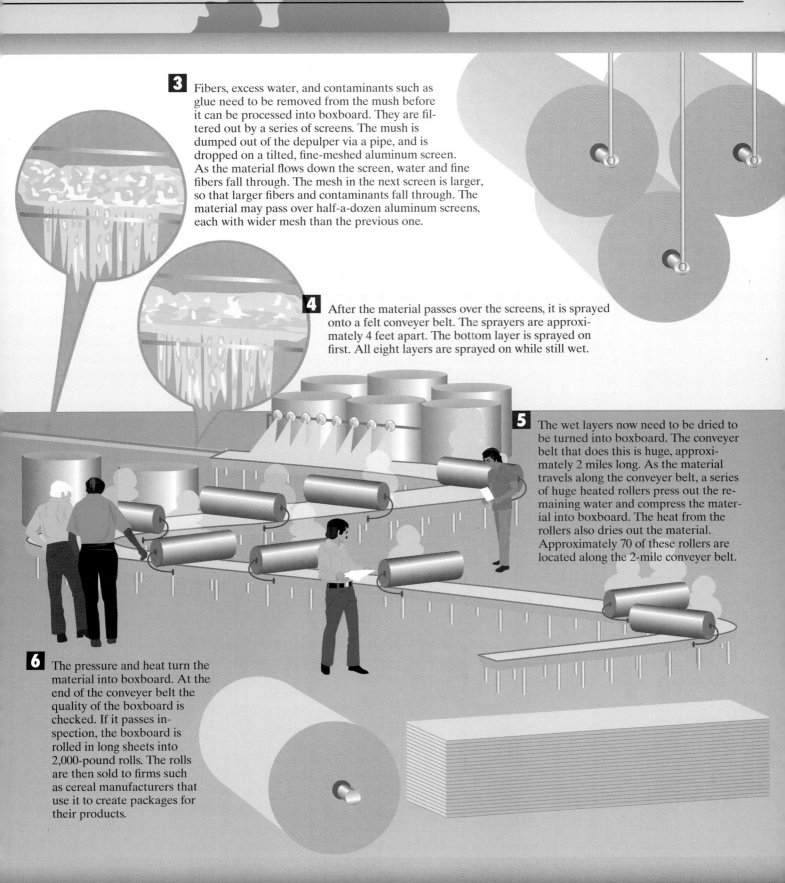

3 Fibers, excess water, and contaminants such as glue need to be removed from the mush before it can be processed into boxboard. They are filtered out by a series of screens. The mush is dumped out of the depulper via a pipe, and is dropped on a tilted, fine-meshed aluminum screen. As the material flows down the screen, water and fine fibers fall through. The mesh in the next screen is larger, so that larger fibers and contaminants fall through. The material may pass over half-a-dozen aluminum screens, each with wider mesh than the previous one.

4 After the material passes over the screens, it is sprayed onto a felt conveyer belt. The sprayers are approximately 4 feet apart. The bottom layer is sprayed on first. All eight layers are sprayed on while still wet.

5 The wet layers now need to be dried to be turned into boxboard. The conveyer belt that does this is huge, approximately 2 miles long. As the material travels along the conveyer belt, a series of huge heated rollers press out the remaining water and compress the material into boxboard. The heat from the rollers also dries out the material. Approximately 70 of these rollers are located along the 2-mile conveyer belt.

6 The pressure and heat turn the material into boxboard. At the end of the conveyer belt the quality of the boxboard is checked. If it passes inspection, the boxboard is rolled in long sheets into 2,000-pound rolls. The rolls are then sold to firms such as cereal manufacturers that use it to create packages for their products.

How Cars Are Recycled

1 Metals of all kinds are frequently recycled from products as diverse as aluminum cans, refrigerators, and entire automobiles. This illustration shows one of many ways in which autos can be recycled. First, the entire automobile is placed in a large device that can shear it, chop it, or shred it into fist-sized chunks—something like a large food processor. Some of these devices can shred an entire car in 20 seconds. If a scrap dealer has shredded the car, the car is shipped to a recycling mill that can recapture the metal within it. If the mill itself has shredded the car, it is then sent along to the next part of the recycling process.

2 The fist-sized chunks of automobile are put on a conveyer belt. Large magnets are suspended above the belt. As the shredded automobile parts make their way down the conveyer belt, the steel is attracted to the magnets. The steel is then taken away for recycling.

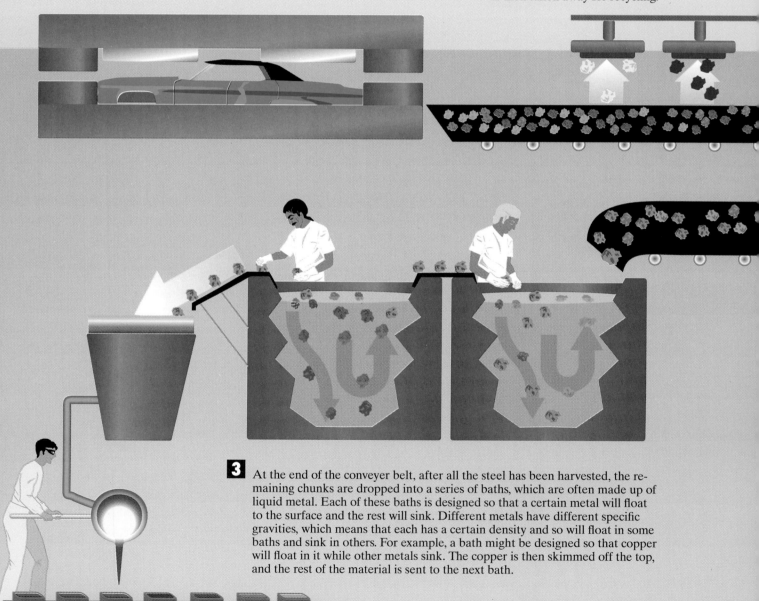

3 At the end of the conveyer belt, after all the steel has been harvested, the remaining chunks are dropped into a series of baths, which are often made up of liquid metal. Each of these baths is designed so that a certain metal will float to the surface and the rest will sink. Different metals have different specific gravities, which means that each has a certain density and so will float in some baths and sink in others. For example, a bath might be designed so that copper will float in it while other metals sink. The copper is then skimmed off the top, and the rest of the material is sent to the next bath.

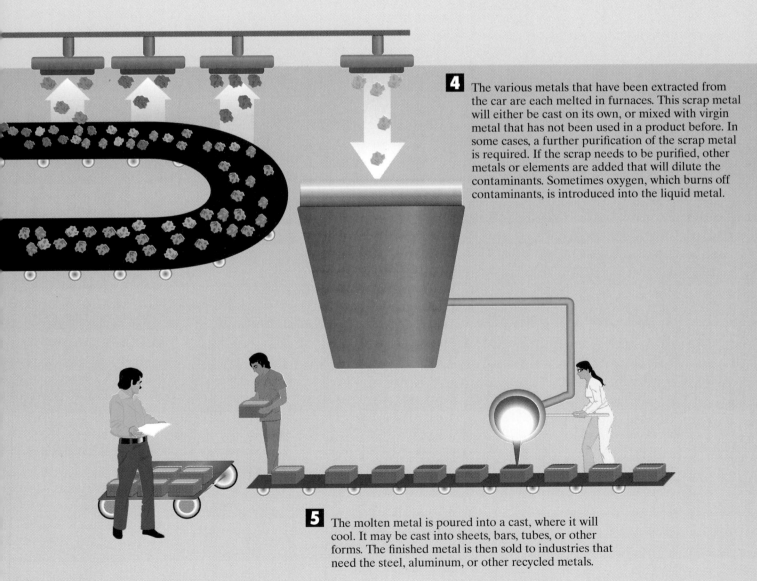

4 The various metals that have been extracted from the car are each melted in furnaces. This scrap metal will either be cast on its own, or mixed with virgin metal that has not been used in a product before. In some cases, a further purification of the scrap metal is required. If the scrap needs to be purified, other metals or elements are added that will dilute the contaminants. Sometimes oxygen, which burns off contaminants, is introduced into the liquid metal.

5 The molten metal is poured into a cast, where it will cool. It may be cast into sheets, bars, tubes, or other forms. The finished metal is then sold to industries that need the steel, aluminum, or other recycled metals.

An Environmentally Friendly Landfill

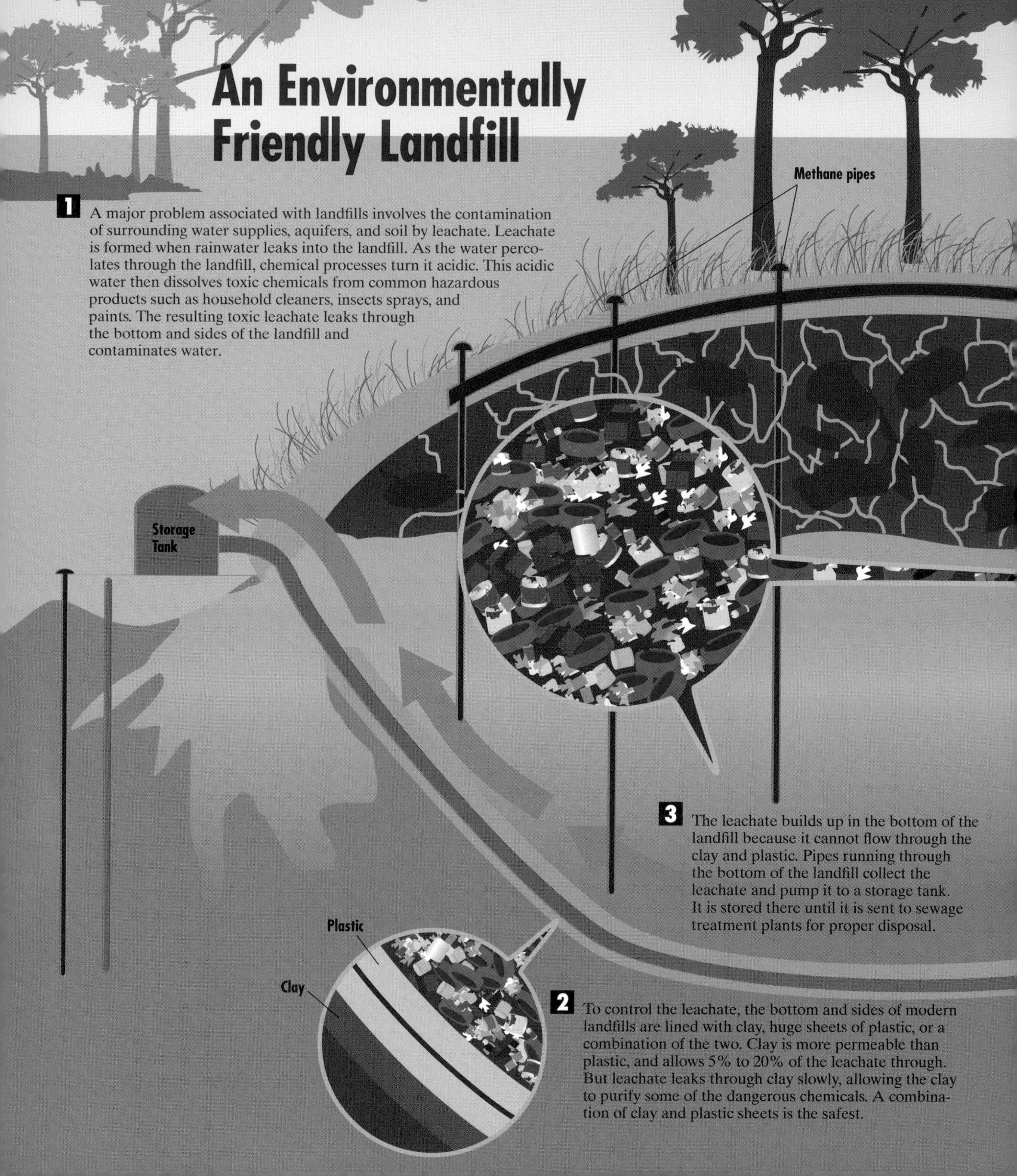

Methane pipes

1 A major problem associated with landfills involves the contamination of surrounding water supplies, aquifers, and soil by leachate. Leachate is formed when rainwater leaks into the landfill. As the water percolates through the landfill, chemical processes turn it acidic. This acidic water then dissolves toxic chemicals from common hazardous products such as household cleaners, insects sprays, and paints. The resulting toxic leachate leaks through the bottom and sides of the landfill and contaminates water.

Storage
Tank

3 The leachate builds up in the bottom of the landfill because it cannot flow through the clay and plastic. Pipes running through the bottom of the landfill collect the leachate and pump it to a storage tank. It is stored there until it is sent to sewage treatment plants for proper disposal.

Plastic

Clay

2 To control the leachate, the bottom and sides of modern landfills are lined with clay, huge sheets of plastic, or a combination of the two. Clay is more permeable than plastic, and allows 5% to 20% of the leachate through. But leachate leaks through clay slowly, allowing the clay to purify some of the dangerous chemicals. A combination of clay and plastic sheets is the safest.

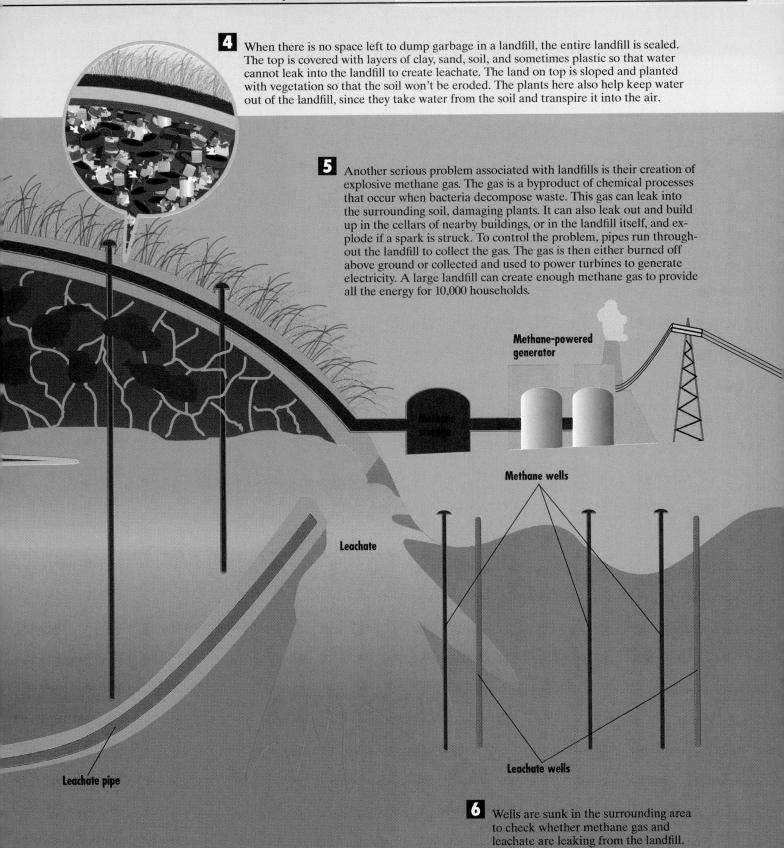

4 When there is no space left to dump garbage in a landfill, the entire landfill is sealed. The top is covered with layers of clay, sand, soil, and sometimes plastic so that water cannot leak into the landfill to create leachate. The land on top is sloped and planted with vegetation so that the soil won't be eroded. The plants here also help keep water out of the landfill, since they take water from the soil and transpire it into the air.

5 Another serious problem associated with landfills is their creation of explosive methane gas. The gas is a byproduct of chemical processes that occur when bacteria decompose waste. This gas can leak into the surrounding soil, damaging plants. It can also leak out and build up in the cellars of nearby buildings, or in the landfill itself, and explode if a spark is struck. To control the problem, pipes run throughout the landfill to collect the gas. The gas is then either burned off above ground or collected and used to power turbines to generate electricity. A large landfill can create enough methane gas to provide all the energy for 10,000 households.

Methane-powered generator

Methane storage

Methane wells

Leachate

Leachate pipe

Leachate wells

6 Wells are sunk in the surrounding area to check whether methane gas and leachate are leaking from the landfill.

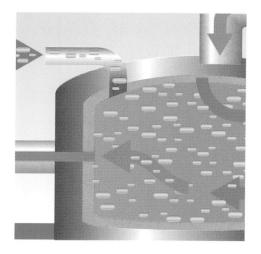

Cleaning Up Hazardous Wastes

THE HEADLINES HAVE become all too common: higher childhood leukemia rates in Woburn, Massachusetts; higher breast cancer rates for women in Long Island, New York; a plethora of horrifying health problems for those living near the infamous Love Canal in upstate New York—all the result of living near chemical plants or hazardous waste dumps. There are few regions that haven't been touched by similar man-made disasters—the Council on Economic Priorities estimates that 80% of people in the United States live somewhere near a hazardous waste site.

Hazardous waste is one of the most frightening and intractable problems caused by industrial societies. These byproducts of manufacturing attack the overall health of the environment as well as human health. In past decades, hazardous wastes were simply dumped into open pits in the ground. Alternatively, they were stored in metal drums that eventually corroded and leaked into the surrounding countryside, or they were pumped untreated into rivers and streams. Today we are paying the price of that neglect, not only in health and environmental problems, but also in taxes. Through the Environmental Protection Agency's (EPA's) Superfund, we are spending billions of dollars every year to clean up old hazardous waste sites.

The amount of hazardous waste generated every year is astounding. According to the EPA, some 195,000 sites generate hazardous waste in the United States, and 300 million to 700 million tons of toxic matter are created every year. The chemical and petroleum industries are the primary producers of hazardous wastes, although many other industries contribute as well.

However, efforts are being made to solve this problem. Some waste is being *reclaimed*—that is, hazardous materials are taken from it and reused. One example of this is recovering lead from automobile batteries. Another is the incineration of some wastes. In many cases, it is stored in regulated landfills and waste sites. In other cases, the waste is treated so that it becomes less hazardous or not hazardous at all.

There are many ways to clean up existing hazardous waste sites. In some instances, the soil is dug up, carted away, and treated elsewhere. Another alternative is to treat the wastes right on the site. Many different techniques are used to treat the hazardous material. They can also be degraded with chemicals or bacteria, or by flushing the material with water so it can be removed from the site and then burning it. Each site is a unique case and requires special attention.

Some intriguing new treatment techniques have been developed recently. Molten Metal Technology in Fall River, Massachusetts is pioneering a technique in which hazardous wastes are dropped into a tank of superhot liquid metal and chemical catalysts. This breaks down wastes into their constituent elements, such as hydrogen, chlorine, and carbon. By adding other material to the mix, the toxic waste can be turned into useful material such as scrap steel or ceramics.

In the long run, the solution is to stop producing so much waste in the first place, which means that we have to consume fewer manufactured goods, especially those that are disposable. This also means that we will need strict regulations on how the waste can be disposed. We have made much progress on regulating waste. However, we must continue these efforts, especially regarding the clean up of existing waste sites. But we still produce far too many wastes. This problem will never go away unless we cut down our consumption of goods and develop manufacturing techniques and practices that are more environmentally friendly.

Using Microorganisms To Clean Up a Hazardous Waste Site

There are many different ways to clean up a hazardous waste site, and no one technique will work in all cases. *Biodegradation* is one especially promising method. This technique uses microorganisms to eat away the waste. Biodegradation works especially well when the waste is either organic or petroleum based. When this method is used at the waste site itself instead of on wastes hauled away from the site, it is referred to as *in situ biodegradation*.

Oxygen

Mixing tanks

Bacteria and nutrients

3 The bacteria-laden water is pumped to a second mixing tank, where oxygen is added. The oxygenated water enriches the environment for the bacteria, allowing the bacteria population to grow even more.

Injection well

Toxic waste

4 The oxygen-rich and bacterially active water, now cleaned by the waste-eating microbes, is injected into the ground above the contaminant source. The water flows through the contaminated soil. As it does so, the bacteria eat away at the waste. The water also flushes waste down toward the extraction well. This water flows into the *leachate plume*, which is the plume of contaminated water flowing through the soil. Bacteria eat the waste in the plume.

Leachate plume

2 Bacteria that eat waste are added to the mixing tank. These bacteria are normally found at the waste site because they are well adapted to local conditions. However, bacteria strains that eat a specific kind of hazardous waste can be grown elsewhere and brought to the site, and bacteria that have been genetically engineered to eat wastes can also be added to the tank. Nutrients, including nitrates and phosphates, are added to the tank to help increase the bacteria population. The bacteria eat at waste in the tank.

Aquifer

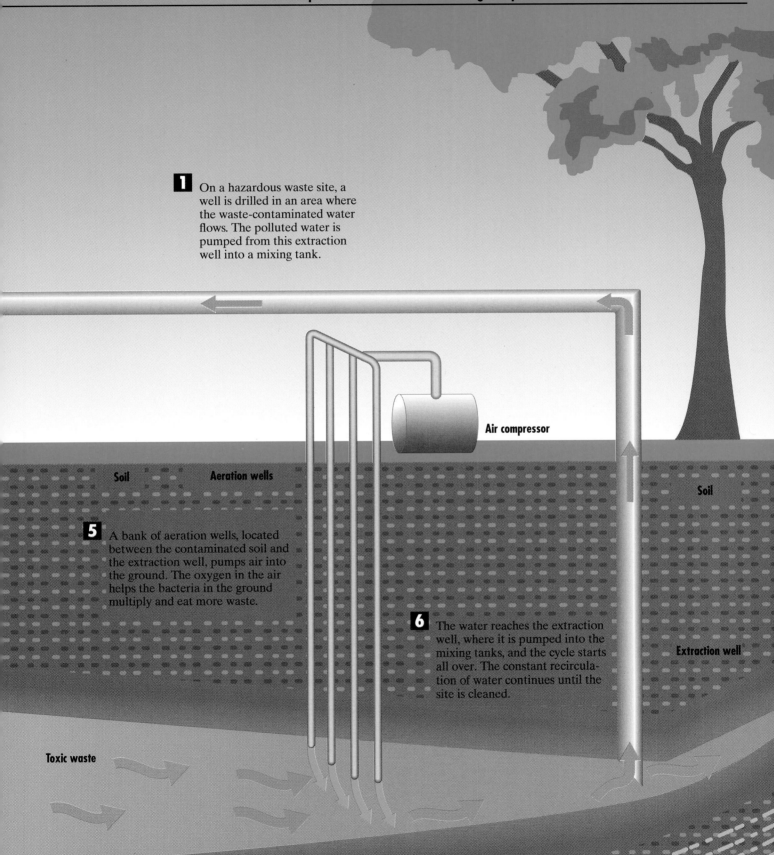

1 On a hazardous waste site, a well is drilled in an area where the waste-contaminated water flows. The polluted water is pumped from this extraction well into a mixing tank.

Air compressor

Soil

Aeration wells

Soil

5 A bank of aeration wells, located between the contaminated soil and the extraction well, pumps air into the ground. The oxygen in the air helps the bacteria in the ground multiply and eat more waste.

6 The water reaches the extraction well, where it is pumped into the mixing tanks, and the cycle starts all over. The constant recirculation of water continues until the site is cleaned.

Extraction well

Toxic waste

Aquifer

OUR POLLUTED AIR

CONTENTS

NOTHING IS QUITE as invigorating as the first breath of fresh air on a cool, spring morning far away from a city. And almost nothing is as unpleasant as waking up to the grayish-yellow blanket of smog that envelops so many of our cities every summer. It's hard to imagine that we have managed to tarnish so much of the vast expanse of sky above us.

We have, though. And the ways in which we have fouled the air pose severe threats to human health, the environment, and the survival of the biosphere. Sometimes the threat is invisible, such as the destruction being wrought on the ozone layer high up in the earth's stratosphere, or the acid rain that falls to earth, killing fish, plants, and entire ponds and lakes. Other times the threat is all too perceivable, such as the smog that envelops many of the world's cities. But there is a common thread to all this deadly destruction: It can all be ameliorated, or even ended. Our collective resolve and cooperation are the major requirements.

The earth's atmosphere is composed of a number of gases and of water vapor. The most common gas is nitrogen, which makes up some 78% of the atmosphere. The next most common gas is oxygen, which makes up 21%. Next comes argon, with 0.93%, then carbon dioxide, with 0.03%. There are also traces of other gases such as neon, methane, hydrogen, helium and krypton.

The atmosphere provides gases such as oxygen and carbon dioxide that all plant and animal life need in order to survive. It is the medium through which the water cycle travels. It traps heat from the sun, keeping the earth warm enough to support life. And it keeps out dangerous ultraviolet rays so that plants and animals are not killed by the harmful effects of solar radiation.

The atmosphere is composed mainly of two layers. The bottom layer, the troposphere, takes up approximately the bottom 7 miles of the atmosphere. About 70% of the air in the atmosphere can be found in this layer. Most pollution takes place in the troposphere. It is here that smog and acid rain are formed, and where greenhouse gases such as carbon dioxide accumulate.

Above the troposphere is the stratosphere, which reaches approximately 70 miles above the earth. We take our toll on the stratosphere, as well; it is in the stratosphere that gases congregate that destroy the ozone layer.

Almost all of the problems having to do with the atmosphere stem from the way we use—and misuse—energy. Acid rain is caused by the burning of fossil fuel such as coal and oil and by coal-burning, electricity-generating industrial plants, especially those that use high-sulfur fuels. Smog is created mainly by automobile exhaust and by industries burning fossil fuels. The greenhouse effect and subsequent global warming also have their origins in the burning of fossil fuels.

Energy is not the only culprit. For example, the ozone layer is being destroyed mainly by chemicals called chlorofluorocarbons that have been used in products as diverse as spray cans and air conditioners. And the greenhouse effect is made worse by deforestation.

Ironically, we have the solutions to these problems because we have created them. Energy conservation alone would go a long way toward solving many of them. Rules requiring even stricter clean air standards would certainly help as well. So would international agreements aimed at reducing various forms of air pollution, since dirty air doesn't stop at a country's border.

In this section we'll look at the most important crises facing the atmosphere today. In reading these chapters, it may be easy to believe that our air is so imperiled that no solution is in sight. But the news is not uniformly grim. If you live in a city that historically has been visited by heavy amounts of smog, especially during the summer months, you may have noticed in the last several years that there's simply less smog around than there used to be in some places. That's because legislation in the United States has gone into effect mandating cleaner-burning automobiles and less pollution coming out of industrial smokestacks. And international agreements phasing out chlorofluorocarbons will ensure that the ozone layer is not completely destroyed.

However, our work is cut out for us. There is still too much smog and acid rain, and the hole in the ozone layer has not been repaired miraculously, nor has the greenhouse effect ceased to exist. The solutions to these problems are not mysteries; we know what must be done. Now we must act.

CHAPTER

13

Smog: The Curse of Civilization

WE'VE ALL SEEN it: The yellowish, orangish, or brownish haze that sits above our cities, smelling foul, making our eyes tear, our noses burn, and our throats itch. Smog. The ever-present fact of urban life in the late twentieth century. While smog is most obvious in cities, the haze of smog can be found almost everywhere on Earth. It has reached the remotest ends of the earth: At times, the haze can even be seen in Antarctica.

Smog is a somewhat generic term. There are two types of smog. Smoke from industrial sources such as coal-burning plants and factories that carries within it small pollution particles and gases constitutes one kind of smog. This smoke mixes with fog and creates a low-lying layer of polluted air close to the earth. Air pollution controls over the past decades have made this kind of smog less common.

The kind of smog that we are all familiar with—the kind that sits as a thick haze over many cities in the summer—is called *photochemical smog*. It forms when various types of air pollution from industry and automobiles mix. When this occurs in the presence of sunlight and heat it causes chemical reactions that create toxic chemicals such as ozone. Because photochemical smog is formed in the presence of heat and sunlight, it is mainly a problem during the summer. Some cities, though, suffer from it year-round because they are warm and sunny all year and are located in valleys or basins that don't allow air pollutants to disperse. Los Angeles and Mexico City are two notorious examples. Smog has become so severe in Mexico City that at times industries are forced to cut back on production, and motorists are urged not to drive.

Smog is composed of a kind of toxic chemical soup with some very dangerous ingredients. An itchy throat is the least of the problems that smog causes. Sulfur dioxide attacks the respiratory system, and can be especially harmful and even deadly to people with cardiovascular and respiratory diseases. Nitrogen oxides irritate the lungs and lower resistance to respiratory infections like the flu. Volatile organic compounds irritate the lungs and eyes and can cause nausea. Ozone is a primary component of smog and the one that causes possibly the most severe health problems. It attacks the cardiopulmonary systems, impairs the functioning of the lungs, and can cause chest pain and pulmonary congestion. Finally, particulates in the air damage lung tissue, may cause cancer, and make worse any existing cardiovascular disease.

Smog is so ever-present that the air quality index (formally called the Pollutants Standard Index, or PSI) is regularly reported as part of the daily weather throughout the United States. To arrive at a day's index in an area, the concentration of a number of dangerous pollutants such as sulfur dioxide, carbon monoxide, ozone, and particulates are averaged. The index ranges from between 0 and 30, which is "Good," to over 300, which is "Hazardous."

In the United States, at least, the smog problem is being attacked. Antipollution measures and enforced air quality standards are forcing industries and cities to take drastic measures to reduce smog, and it's paying off. Public transportation, non–gas-burning automobiles, and "scrubbers" that clean polluted air from factory smokestacks are all helping to curb the problem. And in small ways, each one of us can help: We can give up our addiction to autos and use more public transportation, carpool, bike, or walk, instead of driving. Go ahead and try it: Your lungs will thank you for it.

How Smog Is Created

Nitric oxides react with oxygen in the air and produce nitrogen dioxide (NO_2). Sunlight and the corresponding warmth are conducive to converting nitrogen oxides into nitrogen dioxides. Nitrogen dioxide irritates the lungs, and can cause or exacerbate respiratory diseases such as bronchitis and pneumonia. It can also make people more vulnerable to diseases such as influenza.

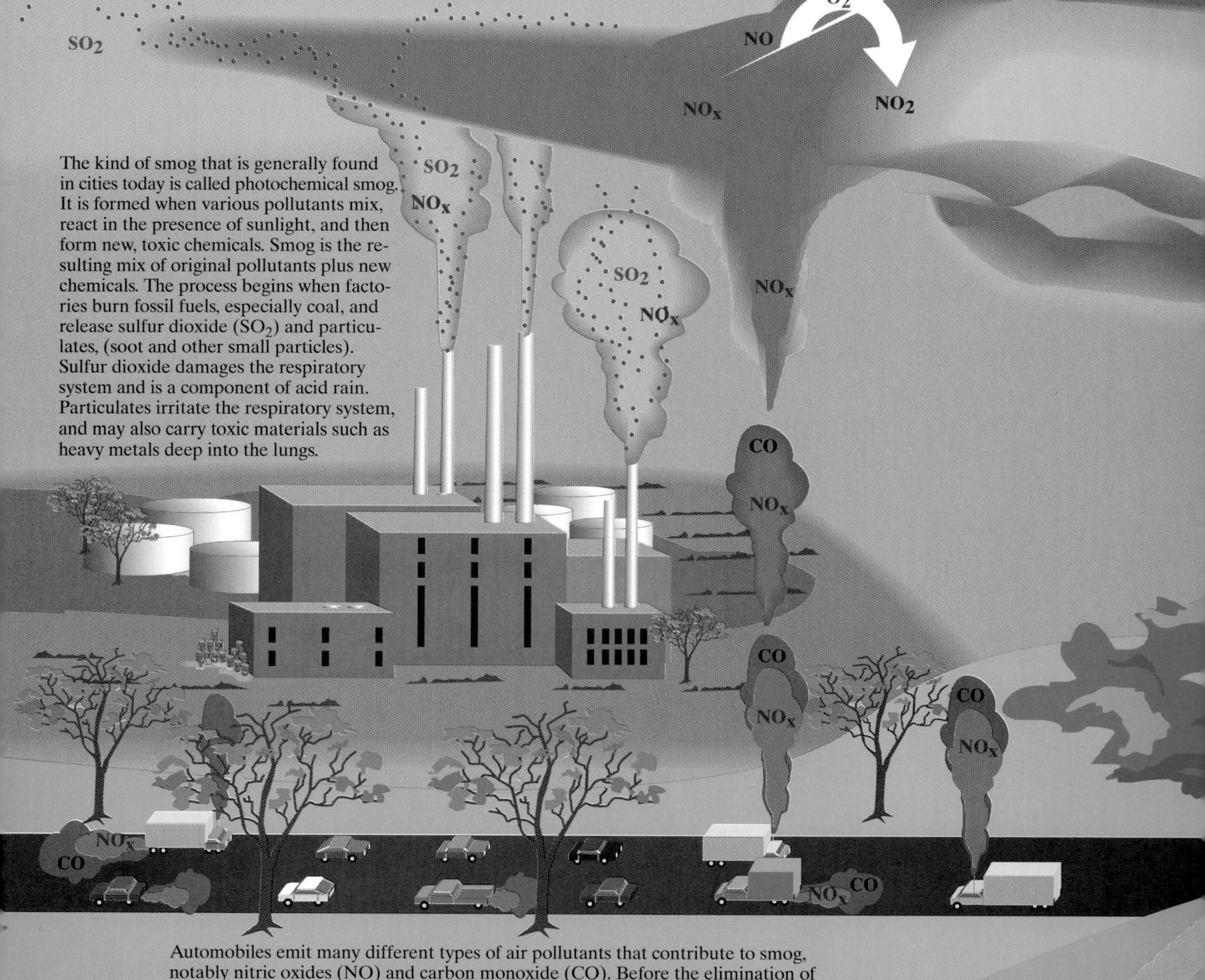

SO_2

O_2

NO

NO_x

NO_2

SO_2
NO_x

SO_2
NO_x

NO_x

The kind of smog that is generally found in cities today is called photochemical smog. It is formed when various pollutants mix, react in the presence of sunlight, and then form new, toxic chemicals. Smog is the resulting mix of original pollutants plus new chemicals. The process begins when factories burn fossil fuels, especially coal, and release sulfur dioxide (SO_2) and particulates, (soot and other small particles). Sulfur dioxide damages the respiratory system and is a component of acid rain. Particulates irritate the respiratory system, and may also carry toxic materials such as heavy metals deep into the lungs.

CO
NO_x

CO
NO_x

CO
NO_x

NO_x
CO

NO_x CO

Automobiles emit many different types of air pollutants that contribute to smog, notably nitric oxides (NO) and carbon monoxide (CO). Before the elimination of lead in gasolines in the United States, much lead was released as well. Carbon monoxide causes drowsiness, lethargy, and headaches, and can also lead to angina attacks. Lead affects the nervous system and lowers children's learning ability.

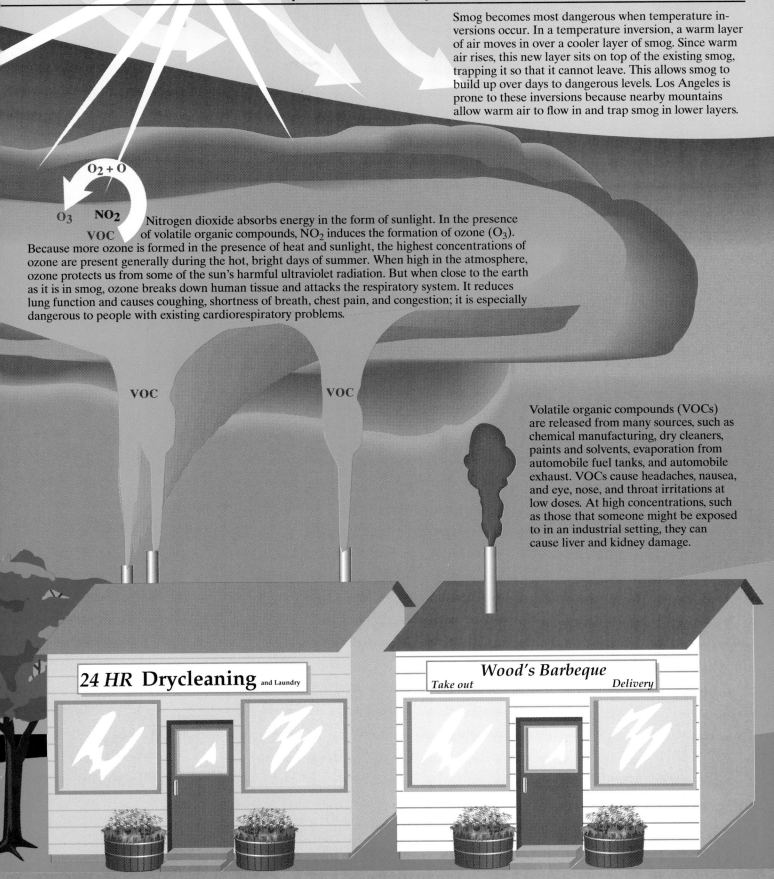

Smog becomes most dangerous when temperature inversions occur. In a temperature inversion, a warm layer of air moves in over a cooler layer of smog. Since warm air rises, this new layer sits on top of the existing smog, trapping it so that it cannot leave. This allows smog to build up over days to dangerous levels. Los Angeles is prone to these inversions because nearby mountains allow warm air to flow in and trap smog in lower layers.

$O_2 + O$

O_3 NO_2

VOC Nitrogen dioxide absorbs energy in the form of sunlight. In the presence of volatile organic compounds, NO_2 induces the formation of ozone (O_3). Because more ozone is formed in the presence of heat and sunlight, the highest concentrations of ozone are present generally during the hot, bright days of summer. When high in the atmosphere, ozone protects us from some of the sun's harmful ultraviolet radiation. But when close to the earth as it is in smog, ozone breaks down human tissue and attacks the respiratory system. It reduces lung function and causes coughing, shortness of breath, chest pain, and congestion; it is especially dangerous to people with existing cardiorespiratory problems.

VOC   VOC

Volatile organic compounds (VOCs) are released from many sources, such as chemical manufacturing, dry cleaners, paints and solvents, evaporation from automobile fuel tanks, and automobile exhaust. VOCs cause headaches, nausea, and eye, nose, and throat irritations at low doses. At high concentrations, such as those that someone might be exposed to in an industrial setting, they can cause liver and kidney damage.

24 HR Drycleaning and Laundry

Wood's Barbeque
Take out   Delivery

The Greenhouse Effect and Global Warming

I S THE EARTH getting warmer? Although some recent frigid winters may convince you otherwise, many scientists say that it is. They note that in this century, the average temperature has already risen by almost 1° Fahrenheit, and that by 2050, it may be 4° warmer.

Many scientists and environmentalists attribute this warming to the greenhouse effect. This occurs when "greenhouse" gases, such as carbon dioxide and methane, rise into the atmosphere and trap the heat reflected from sunlight striking the earth. This heat is then reflected back toward earth, warming the planet. Without those gases, the heat would radiate out into space. A certain concentration of greenhouse gases is necessary to keep the earth warm. Recently, however, the concentration of greenhouse gases has risen rapidly due to human activities—possibly leading to global warming. The primary greenhouse gas, carbon dioxide, is created by the burning of fossil fuels. And more carbon dioxide is present in the atmosphere than ever before because plants and trees, which normally take in carbon dioxide and release oxygen, are being cut down. Ozone, another greenhouse gas, is also created by pollution.

If the earth is, in fact, becoming warmer, it will mean more than steamier summers. The polar ice caps may melt, causing seas to rise and causing flooding in coastal cities. More droughts may occur and more deserts may be created, leading to mass starvation. The earth will not warm equally; the poles are expected to warm more than the middle of the earth. This will cause drastic climatic changes, and the kinds of food that can be grown in agricultural regions today will change. Agriculture will shift throughout the world. Because agricultural pests and diseases thrive in warmer weather, there may be much more crop damage. Some scientists believe that climate change will favor the most common plant species, killing off rarer plant forms, so there will be less biodiversity. Weather patterns throughout the world will alter, possibly leading to more extreme weather such as hurricanes and storm surges along the coasts.

Not everyone agrees that the earth is getting warmer. Many believe that it is not. At the moment, there is no way to prove or disprove the theory. The problem, though, is this: If, in fact, it is getting warmer, by the time the evidence proves conclusively that it is happening, it will be too late to do anything about it; the drastic effects will have already taken hold.

O₃

CFC

The Greenhouse Effect and Global Warming

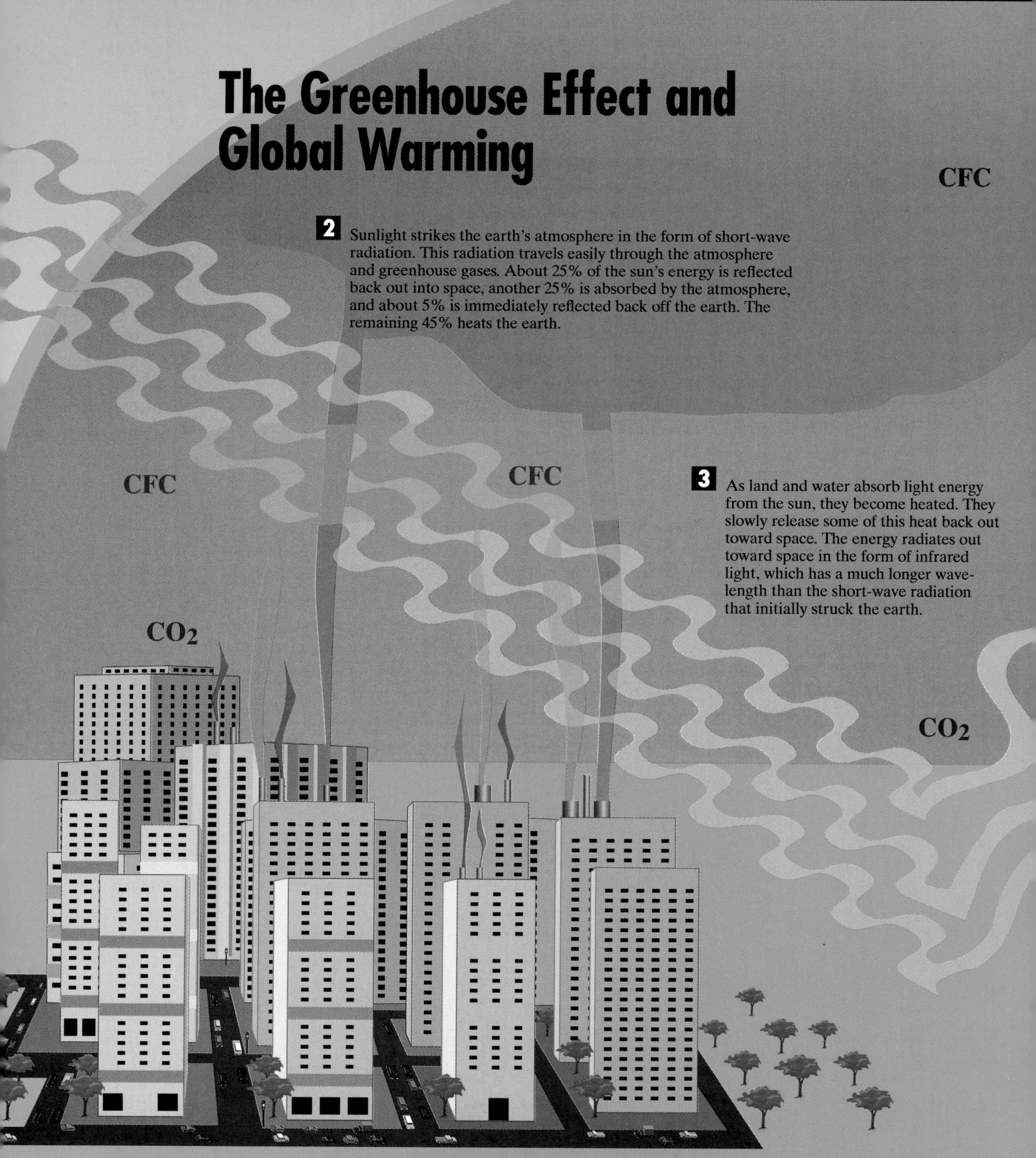

2 Sunlight strikes the earth's atmosphere in the form of short-wave radiation. This radiation travels easily through the atmosphere and greenhouse gases. About 25% of the sun's energy is reflected back out into space, another 25% is absorbed by the atmosphere, and about 5% is immediately reflected back off the earth. The remaining 45% heats the earth.

CFC

CFC

3 As land and water absorb light energy from the sun, they become heated. They slowly release some of this heat back out toward space. The energy radiates out toward space in the form of infrared light, which has a much longer wavelength than the short-wave radiation that initially struck the earth.

CO_2

CO_2

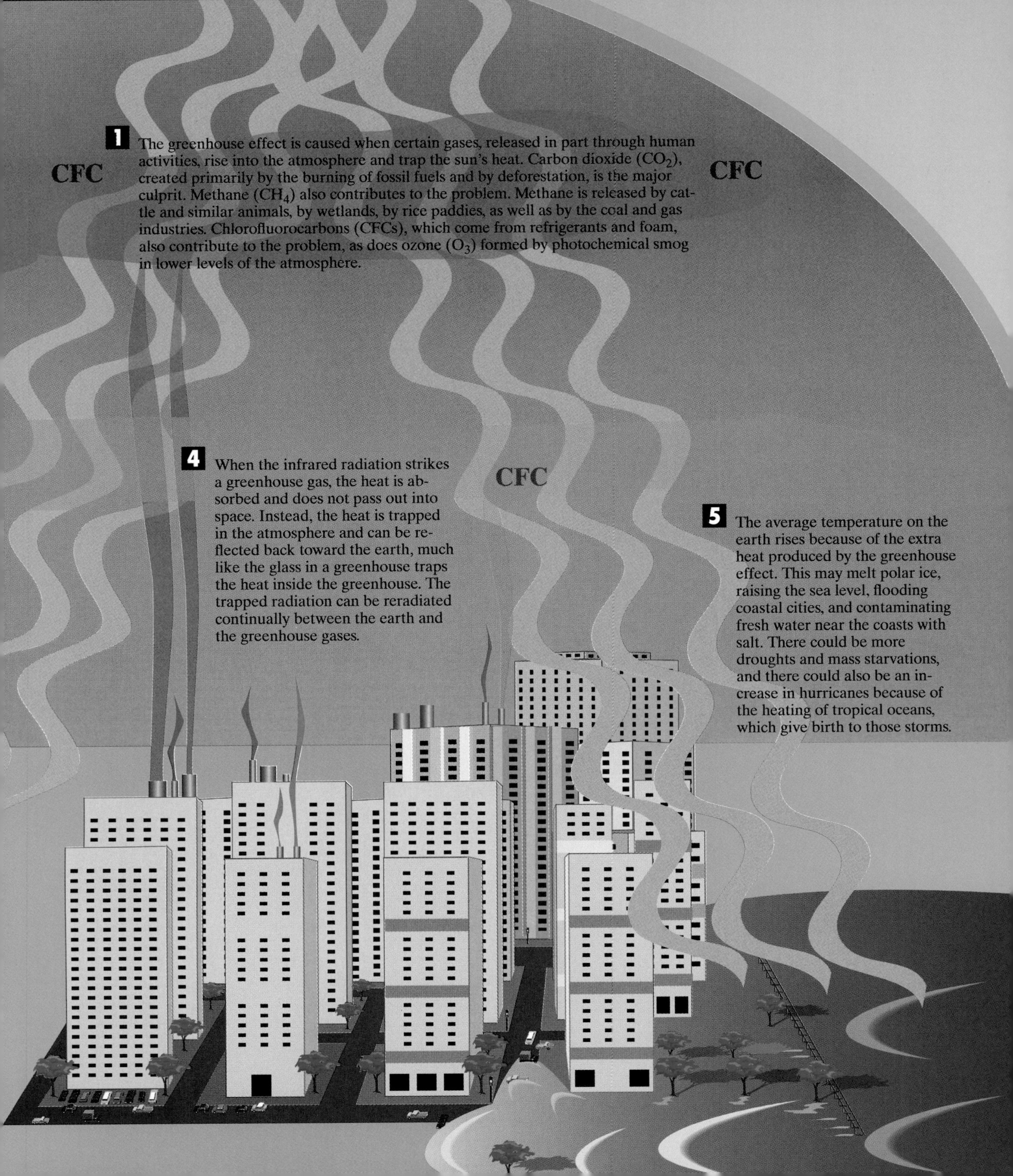

CFC

CFC

1 The greenhouse effect is caused when certain gases, released in part through human activities, rise into the atmosphere and trap the sun's heat. Carbon dioxide (CO_2), created primarily by the burning of fossil fuels and by deforestation, is the major culprit. Methane (CH_4) also contributes to the problem. Methane is released by cattle and similar animals, by wetlands, by rice paddies, as well as by the coal and gas industries. Chlorofluorocarbons (CFCs), which come from refrigerants and foam, also contribute to the problem, as does ozone (O_3) formed by photochemical smog in lower levels of the atmosphere.

4 When the infrared radiation strikes a greenhouse gas, the heat is absorbed and does not pass out into space. Instead, the heat is trapped in the atmosphere and can be reflected back toward the earth, much like the glass in a greenhouse traps the heat inside the greenhouse. The trapped radiation can be reradiated continually between the earth and the greenhouse gases.

CFC

5 The average temperature on the earth rises because of the extra heat produced by the greenhouse effect. This may melt polar ice, raising the sea level, flooding coastal cities, and contaminating fresh water near the coasts with salt. There could be more droughts and mass starvations, and there could also be an increase in hurricanes because of the heating of tropical oceans, which give birth to those storms.

The Ozone Crisis: A Hole in the Sky

EVERY SPRING, A massive, invisible hole three times the size of the United States opens up high in the sky over Antarctica. This hole in the sky allows dangerous ultraviolet radiation to infiltrate the earth below it. Ozone is destroyed in other places above the earth, not just in Antarctica. But a peculiar set of circumstances makes the problem much more severe in Antarctica. During the Antarctic winter, chlorofluorocarbons (CFCs) and other ozone-depleting chemicals accumulate on ice crystals in the atmosphere there. In the spring, when the sun shines and warms the atmosphere, the chemicals start a massive depletion of ozone. After two to three months, the ozone-depleting air mass moves from Antarctica to other parts of the world.

This infamous hole exists in the ozone layer of the earth's atmosphere. CFCs create this hole when they drift upward from the earth into the stratosphere 10 to 30 miles above the earth, and destroy the ozone layer that shields us from ultraviolet radiation. It is a well-known fact that CFCs are the primary culprit responsible for destroying the ozone layer. These gases come from aerosol sprays, coolants for refrigerators and air conditioners, and chemicals used to produce plastic foam. Depending on how it was produced, a single polystyrene cup can contain one billion molecules of CFCs. However, they are not the only gases responsible for ozone destruction. Methyl chloroform, which is used in solvents and as fire retardants, and nitric oxides, which come from automobile combustion, fertilizer, and other sources, are also responsible for the depletion of the ozone layer.

The environmental and health consequences of the depletion of the ozone layer are not immediately visible. While these consequences are not as overtly dramatic as air or water pollution, they are severe. When more ultraviolet radiation makes its way to earth as the result of ozone depletion, it causes skin cancer. It has been estimated that for every 1% of ozone depleted, there is an increase of about 3% in non-melanoma skin cancer. So a 10% reduction of the ozone layer could cause 160,000 cases of this kind of disease in the United States alone.

Cancers are not the only health problem caused by ozone depletion; the incidence of cataracts also increases. The Environmental Protection Agency (EPA) estimates that a 10% reduction of the ozone layer by the year 2050 would lead to 4 million additional cases of cataracts in the United States. The escaped radiation may also suppress the immune system, leading to more cases of infectious diseases.

Humans are not the only victims of ozone depletion. Plants are also damaged by the ultraviolet rays. Plankton in the ocean are killed, and because these form the bottom of the ocean's food chain, all life in the ocean may be affected.

The problem is so severe that we have begun to act on it out of necessity. CFCs and other ozone-depleting chemicals are being phased out all over the world. An international agreement calls for a ban on production of all CFCs and other ozone-depleting chemicals in industrial nations by the year 2000. Developing nations will ban them by the year 2010. Perhaps the ban is not coming soon enough, but the fact that the ban will take effect means that the entire world, for once, has recognized that it must face an environmental threat not individually, but as a whole. And that bodes well for the future cooperative solution of other environmental dangers.

How the Ozone Layer Is Destroyed

1 Although ozone in the lower atmosphere is an air pollutant, a thin layer of ozone and oxygen in the stratosphere 10 to 30 miles above the earth shields us from the sun's harmful ultraviolet rays. It accomplishes this by absorbing the rays. The process starts when ultraviolet radiation strikes a molecule of oxygen (O_2). The oxygen molecule absorbs the ultraviolet energy and splits into two oxygen (O) atoms. These oxygen atoms then each react with molecules of oxygen, forming ozone (O_3) molecules.

2 The ozone molecule now absorbs more ultraviolet light, and splits into an oxygen molecule and an oxygen atom. More ultraviolet light then strikes the oxygen molecule, which absorbs the light and starts the process of creating ozone all over again. Ozone is constantly being created and broken down high above the earth, and in the chemical process of doing this, it absorbs dangerous ultraviolet rays.

3 Chlorofluorocarbons (CFCs) drift upward from the surface of the earth to the ozone layer. These gases come from many sources, notably aerosol cans, refrigerator and air conditioner coolant, and from the manufacture of plastic foams.

⊙	**Oxygen atom**
⊙⊙	**Oxygen molecule**
⊙⊙	**Ozone**
Cl C F Cl Cl	**Chlorofluorocarbon molecule**
Cl	**Chlorine atom**
Cl O	**Chlorine monoxide**

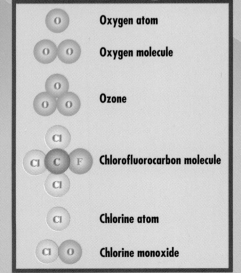

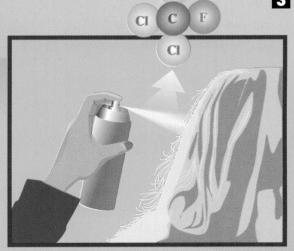

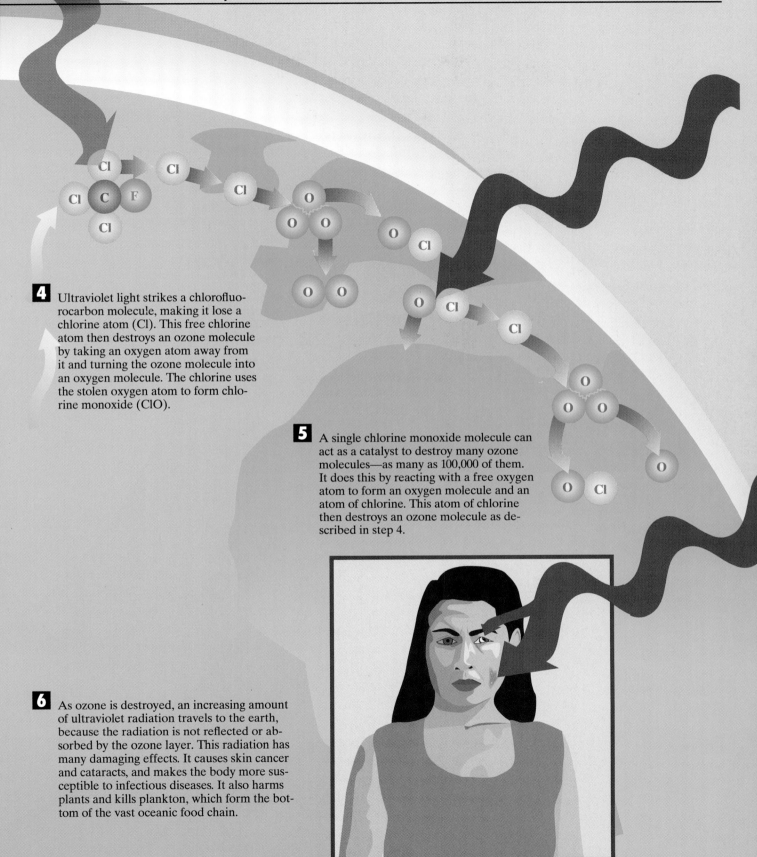

4 Ultraviolet light strikes a chlorofluorocarbon molecule, making it lose a chlorine atom (Cl). This free chlorine atom then destroys an ozone molecule by taking an oxygen atom away from it and turning the ozone molecule into an oxygen molecule. The chlorine uses the stolen oxygen atom to form chlorine monoxide (ClO).

5 A single chlorine monoxide molecule can act as a catalyst to destroy many ozone molecules—as many as 100,000 of them. It does this by reacting with a free oxygen atom to form an oxygen molecule and an atom of chlorine. This atom of chlorine then destroys an ozone molecule as described in step 4.

6 As ozone is destroyed, an increasing amount of ultraviolet radiation travels to the earth, because the radiation is not reflected or absorbed by the ozone layer. This radiation has many damaging effects. It causes skin cancer and cataracts, and makes the body more susceptible to infectious diseases. It also harms plants and kills plankton, which form the bottom of the vast oceanic food chain.

Acid Rain

ACID PRECIPITATION, or *acid rain*, is perhaps the most insidious form of environmental destruction. It causes widespread damage to lakes, forests, and wildlife, as well as to man-made structures. Acid rain turns lakes acidic, killing off the fish populations and other waterlife. It disrupts the bottom of the food chain so that bird populations decrease—the birds' food supply becomes depleted when acid rain kills off insects, plants, and other water wildlife. In Germany, acid rain is implicated in *Waldsterben*, the destruction of forests. It also leaches heavy toxic metals out of the soil and into lakes, streams, and public water supplies, and it damages statues and public buildings. Acid rain may even be responsible for certain health problems.

Sulfur dioxide and nitric oxides are air pollutants. When they mix with moisture in the atmosphere to form acids, acid rain results. Prevailing winds transport the acid, and acid rain falls, either in the form of precipitation or dry particles. Acid rain can fall as far away as 2,500 miles from the original source of pollution. The smokestacks and automobiles of the industrial heartland of the Midwest have caused the acid rain that is bedeviling the eastern United States and northeastern Canada. Acid rain falling in Scandinavia comes largely from European sources to the west, the United Kingdom in particular.

The areas that receive acid rain are not equally affected by it. A region's ability to neutralize acids determines the amount of potential damage. Alkaline soil neutralizes acid. Therefore, areas with highly alkaline soils—such as the Midwest—suffer less damage than those areas where the soil is either neutral or acidic, such as eastern North America.

Some stopgap measures have been tried to solve the problem. Adding lime to polluted lakes in an attempt to neutralize the acid in them is an example of this. However, such measures haven't worked. Trying to solve the acid-rain problem this way is like using a Band-Aid to try to stem the blood flowing from a severed artery. The real solution is to drastically cut down on the pollutants that cause acid rain. This means drastically cutting our reliance on fossil fuels such as coal, especially high-sulfur coal. It also means dramatically reducing emissions from automobiles through conservation, the use of alternate energy, and greater use of mass transit. The problem won't be solved until these steps are taken.

How Acid Rain Is Formed and Its Environmental Effects

1 The air pollutants sulfur dioxide and nitric oxide are the two main culprits in the formation of acid rain. When fossil fuel—especially high-sulfur coal—is burned in electricity-generating plants and other industrial sites in the Midwest, sulfur dioxide is spewed into the atmosphere from the tops of high smokestacks. Nitric oxide is emitted into the atmosphere primarily from automobiles. Prevailing winds transport both of these pollutants.

2 As the prevailing winds transport sulfur dioxide and nitric oxide, these pollutants react with water in the atmosphere to form sulfuric acid and nitric acid.

4 In areas where the soil is highly alkaline, or where there is limestone bedrock, the alkalinity in the soil and limestone neutralize the acid rain. Under these circumstances, there are no major environmental effects.

(+) Alkaline	(−) Acid	▼ Sulfur dioxide ▼ Nitric oxide
Moisture (H₂0)	Sulfuric acid	Nitric acid

3 Rain, snow, and other precipitation containing sulfuric and nitric acids fall to the earth as the acids travel. Dry, acidic particles fall as well. An Environmental Protection Agency (EPA) study has found the average acidity of rain and snow over the eastern United States to be at a pH level of around 4.5, over ten times as acidic as normal rain. In Pennsylvania, precipitation has been measured to be as acidic as vinegar. Wheeling, West Virginia once had rainfall that was nearly as acidic as battery acid.

5 Acid can't be neutralized in areas that contain granite bedrock, or in places where the soil is neutral or acidic. When lakes become acidic, fish and amphibians have a difficult time reproducing. Larvae and *fingerlings*—young, small fish—are killed off, further reducing the fish population and disrupting the food chain so that larger fish and birds cannot survive. Some mature fish are killed as well, not just by the acidic environment, but also by heavy toxic metals that the acid has leached out of the surrounding soil into lakes.

6 The ways in which acid rain damages forests are not entirely understood. However, many environmentalists believe that acid damages leaf surfaces, and some species of trees appear not be able to retain water because of this. Acid leaches vital nutrients such as calcium, magnesium, and potassium from the soil and from the trees themselves. Acid also frees toxic metals such as aluminum from the soil. These metals can damage roots and cause further harm to forests.

Physician's Waiting Room: Please Be Seated

7 Acid leaches heavy toxic metals into public water supplies. The acid also erodes statues, monuments, and buildings; it even eats away paint. Acids in the air may contribute to respiratory diseases, especially in children. Acid rain may also harm crop production.

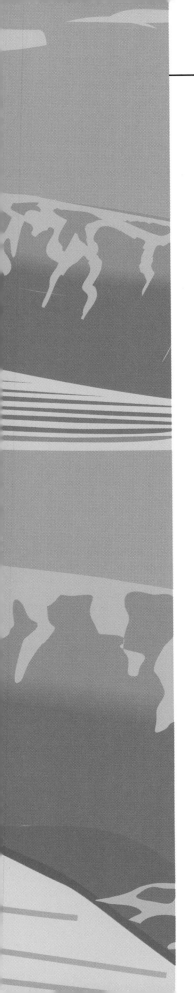

OCEANS: THE SOURCE OF LIFE

4

CONTENTS

WE LIVE IN a watery world. Oceans cover over two-thirds of the earth's surface, and to a great degree they are responsible for sustaining all life. The oceans gave birth to the first living things on earth some 4 billion years ago. They have helped nourish all life since that time, as a food source and as a vital link in global ecological cycles. They supply us with rain, they supply us with food, they help regulate our climate, they drive our weather, and they help ensure that carbon dioxide and oxygen remain in balance. Oceans help regulate the greenhouse effect—billions of its tiny plants called phytoplankton absorb the greenhouse gas carbon dioxide and release oxygen. We can thank the oceans for the air that we breathe, because these phytoplankton are responsible for creating from one-third to one-half of all the oxygen in our atmosphere. And the oceans have given more than a few of us spiritual inspiration as well. So it's no accident that so much of the world's population lives near the oceans. According to the United Nations, six out of every ten people on the planet live near the coast.

It should be a matter of course that we would treat the ocean with the utmost respect and care. Sadly, that isn't the case. We pollute. We overfish. We treat the oceans as a dump and assume that we can keep abusing them forever, with no fear of consequences.

However, consequences materialize with a vengeance. We are paying the debt that is being exacted by centuries of abuse and neglect of this vast resource. We have so overfished some parts of the ocean that what once seemed inexhaustible reserves are now in danger of becoming barren. The unthinkable has happened in New England, for example: A thriving fishing industry has become decimated because the stocks of fish off George's Banks and other traditional fishing areas are so depleted that fishing had to be significantly curtailed there. Salmon fisheries of the Pacific Northwest have been depleted as well.

Stories of refuse and medical waste washing up on beaches have become all too common. So have devastating oil spills. Much of our coasts are polluted and unswimmable. And the hidden consequences are even worse: We have upset the exquisite balance of the ocean's ecosystem.

The oceanic ecosystem is a mystery to most of us, because it is one we rarely see. In some ways, it mirrors the land's ecosystem. As on land, all life in the oceans is supported by a vast food web. At the bottom of that web are phytoplankton that live on the energy of the sun and nutrients. Tiny animals called zooplankton feed upon them, and then larger sea animals feed upon the zooplankton, which in turn are eaten by even larger sea animals. Dead plant and animal matter sinks to the bottom of the sea, where it is fed upon by scavengers such as crabs. Other microorganisms also feed on the matter and degrade it into nutrients that phytoplankton can use.

The coasts are the richest sources of oceanic life; 90% of all fish caught in the ocean are caught in the third of the ocean that is closest to the coastlines. Coasts are also where most of the oceanic nutrients can be found. Many of these nutrients are carried to the coasts by upwellings of current from the ocean floor. Many more come from the land, where rivers, streams, and estuaries wash nutrients from the land into the ocean. Coasts are endangered because they are overdeveloped, which destroys vital links in the oceanic ecosystem.

Rivers can carry nutrients into the oceans. Unfortunately, they also carry pollutants, which pose the greatest danger to the oceans. One way or another, much of the pollution produced on land ends up in the sea. Sewage, industrial wastes, urban runoff, agricultural runoff, and even acid rain contribute to the fouling of the oceans, especially the coasts.

Luckily, the oceans are not so far gone that they cannot be saved. A number of international agreements and agencies have attempted to save the oceans and their inhabitants. For example, the International Whaling Commission outlawed whaling in 1986, and most countries in the years since have agreed to stop killing whales. The International Convention of the Prevention of Pollution from Ships (called MARPOL) has attempted to regulate and even prohibit the discharge of oil, garbage, and other pollution by ships. The Barcelona Convention has been attempting to clean up the fouled Mediterranean since 1976. And many other national and international treaties and organizations are attacking this problem.

Many of these efforts are little more than stopgap measures. We need to change the way we regard the oceans in order to protect them. We must realize that they are not limitless resources that can be infinitely abused. They are finite resources that need very special care.

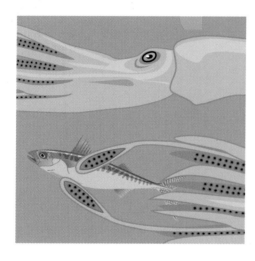

The Ocean's Ecosystem

WHEN WE LOOK out at the ocean, we see a vast, placid place, largely devoid of life, but remarkable life forms teem beneath the waves. The ocean is home to an incredibly rich ecosystem, as complex as the one we see around us on land.

The ocean's food chain is very much like a pyramid of numbers; larger quantities of food are needed to support the animals at each step up. For example, it takes 10,000 pounds of a kind of phytoplankton called a diatom to sustain 1,000 pounds of a zooplankton called a copepod. It takes some 1,000 pounds of copepods to sustain 10 pounds of mackerel. Ten pounds of mackerel sustain one pound of tuna, and so on up to the top of the food chain.

Most of that life is not to be found out in the open ocean, or deep beneath the ocean's surface. Instead, it thrives in shallow coastal areas, and close to the surface. The open sea covers 90% of the ocean's total area, but it contains only 10% of its plant and animal life. That's because in the sea, just as on land, the sun is the engine that drives all of life. Sunlight penetrates only the ocean's surface, where tiny one-celled plants called *phytoplankton* turn it into energy and form the base of the ocean's food chain. Phytoplankton serve another, more global purpose as well. They help to maintain the balance between carbon dioxide and oxygen in our atmosphere by taking in vast amounts of carbon dioxide and releasing huge amounts of oxygen during photosynthesis.

Phytoplankton are eaten by tiny animals called *zooplankton.* Zooplankton are then consumed by anchovies, sardines, and other small surface-feeding fish. These fish are, in turn, preyed upon by larger fish such as tuna, who are then eaten by sharks and other larger fish. Bottom-dwelling creatures feed on organic debris that falls to the ocean floor.

Marine organisms are like land plants and animals in that they are specially suited to certain niches. They have adapted to certain light, water pressure, and temperature conditions. Most are cold-blooded. In temperate regions, where the salinity and temperature of the water change throughout the year, there are fewer species than in nontemperate zones. But there tend to be larger populations of each species in temperate zones.

It is easy to forget how we have endangered the ocean's ecosystem, because we rarely see the creatures in it, except occasionally on our dinner table or at an aquarium. Not only have we used the ocean as a dumping ground, it is also the place where waterborne wastes end up, so its ecosystem has certainly been put at risk. Ironically, only by cleaning up the land, rivers, and streams will we ensure a clean, thriving ocean as well.

The Ocean's Ecosystem

1 Nearly all life in our planet's vast oceans is supported by billions of microscopic phytoplankton that live in the top layer of the ocean. Phytoplankton are a class of minute, one-celled plants that serve the same function as plants do on the land: to convert the energy of the sunlight into living matter and to form the bottom of the food chain. Photosynthesis and ingesting nutrients that wash up from the floor of the ocean cause them to grow. A cubic meter of ocean water can contain as many as 200,000 phytoplankton.

2 Phytoplankton are fed upon by zooplankton, a name that encompasses a great many forms of ocean life. At times, zooplankton even feed upon each other. Zooplankton include krill (shrimp-like creatures); copepods; the larvae of animals such as worms and crabs; young fish called fish fry; and many other kinds of small animals.

5 Nutrient-rich debris from dead animals, food scraps, and dead plants drop toward the bottom of the ocean. Scavengers, such as the eel-like hagfish, and bottom dwellers, such as crabs, sea urchins, and sponges, live off of this debris. What is not eaten by scavengers and other creatures is decomposed by bacteria on the ocean floor and turned into nutrients.

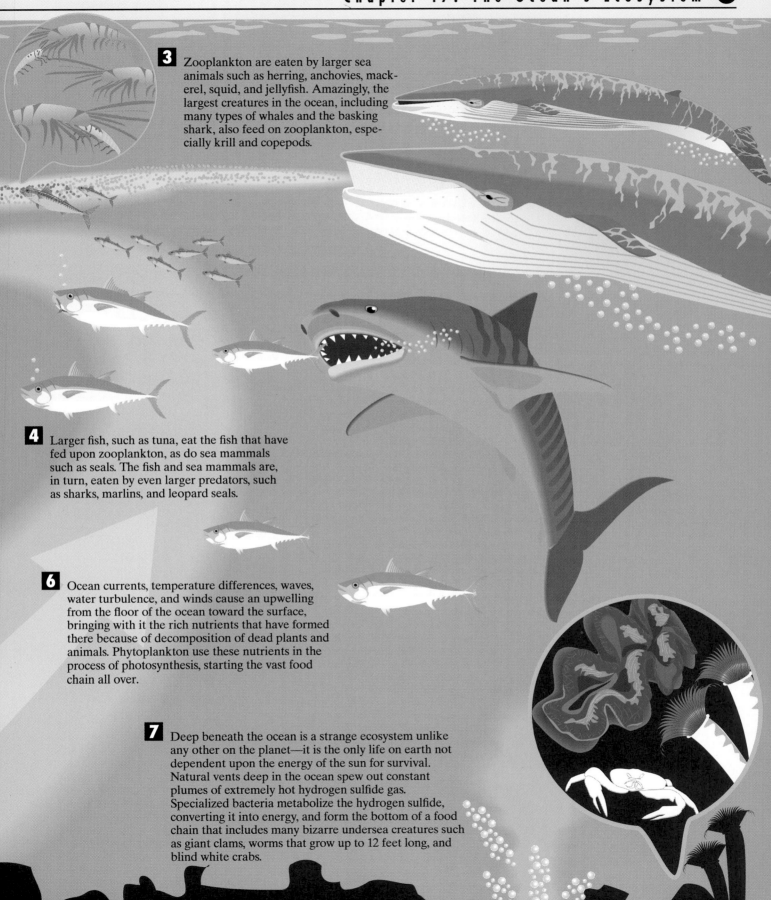

3 Zooplankton are eaten by larger sea animals such as herring, anchovies, mackerel, squid, and jellyfish. Amazingly, the largest creatures in the ocean, including many types of whales and the basking shark, also feed on zooplankton, especially krill and copepods.

4 Larger fish, such as tuna, eat the fish that have fed upon zooplankton, as do sea mammals such as seals. The fish and sea mammals are, in turn, eaten by even larger predators, such as sharks, marlins, and leopard seals.

6 Ocean currents, temperature differences, waves, water turbulence, and winds cause an upwelling from the floor of the ocean toward the surface, bringing with it the rich nutrients that have formed there because of decomposition of dead plants and animals. Phytoplankton use these nutrients in the process of photosynthesis, starting the vast food chain all over.

7 Deep beneath the ocean is a strange ecosystem unlike any other on the planet—it is the only life on earth not dependent upon the energy of the sun for survival. Natural vents deep in the ocean spew out constant plumes of extremely hot hydrogen sulfide gas. Specialized bacteria metabolize the hydrogen sulfide, converting it into energy, and form the bottom of a food chain that includes many bizarre undersea creatures such as giant clams, worms that grow up to 12 feet long, and blind white crabs.

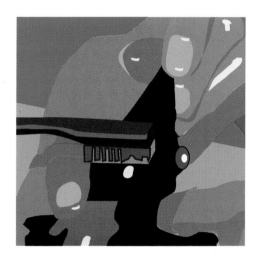

Anatomy of an Oil Spill

FEW ENVIRONMENTAL CATASTROPHES are quite as dramatic as a massive oil spill at sea. In the aftermath of this type of environmental disaster, the grim-looking sea and oil-soaked beaches look as if they can ever be cleaned up, and birds and sea mammals die by the thousands. The infamous *Exxon Valdez* poured 11 million gallons of crude oil into Alaska's Prince William Sound in 1989. This is only the latest catastrophe in a long line of spills of this magnitude. For example, in 1978, the *Amoco Cadiz* ran aground off the Brittany coast in France, spilling eight times the amount of oil spilled by the *Exxon Valdez* and fouling some 200 miles of the French coast.

Cleaning up after a massive oil spill is much like waging a war. It not only requires the front-line soldiers to do the dirty work of ridding the environment of oil, but it also requires massive planning, logistics, and support staffs. And the cleanup is often chaotic. By almost all accounts, the attempt to rid Prince William Sound and environs of oil did not go smoothly because of slow reaction times and poor coordination.

Oil spills do their environmental damage by poisoning the food chain and the environment in general, but they present a particular hazard to birds and mammals. When oil adheres to a bird's feathers or a mammal's fur, it inhibits their normal insulation, and the animals freeze to death.

The environmental damage wrought by oil spills is acute in the short term, though the impact does diminish over time. Tides, wind, and waves all work their natural magic to disperse and break down the oil. Bacteria feed on the oil as well. Nature may be battered, but it survives.

Oil spills are like many other things in life: An ounce of prevention is better than a pound of cure. If tankers were required to have double hulls, spills would be cut dramatically. The *Exxon Valdez* catastrophe, for example, would almost certainly have been averted if this precaution had been taken. Escort vessels accompanying tankers through congested waterways would prevent tankers from grounding. Better traffic control systems would prevent conditions that lead to collisions and other accidents. Keeping tankers far offshore whenever possible would mean that spills would get a chance to disperse before hitting the vulnerable coast and beaches.

But we remain shortsighted in all this: These preventive measures are still not required by law. And massive oil spills are treated as accidents when, in fact, they are anything but accidental. Oil spills are inevitable—accidents waiting to happen—and will continue to be unless we reform the way we ship oil.

An Oil Spill's Environmental Effects

1 When oil spills from the side of a tanker it starts to spread along the ocean's surface. Some of it evaporates. As some of the compounds in the oil evaporate, the oil gets thicker. Waves batter this viscous oil into a thick water-and-oil emulsion called *mousse*. Some mousse washes ashore, while some sinks to the bottom of the ocean. Eventually, the mousse on the surface is sheared into pancake-sized pieces, and then later into tarballs.

2 Seabirds are among a spill's first victims. Some birds get oiled by landing or swimming in water that has oil in it, while other birds become covered with oil when the oil washes ashore. Oil takes away the insulating ability of a bird's feathers, so birds that have been coated with oil—especially in cold regions—die quickly of hypothermia; they freeze to death.

4 Oil disrupts the ocean's food chain by setting of a fatal domino effect. Oil kills the zooplankton that are near the bottom of the chain. Animals and young fish such as fish fry feed upon the zooplankton. With fewer zooplankton to eat, fish fry die, so less fish reach maturity. The fish predators that live off the fish fry have less to eat as well, and their population declines. Sea mammals that feed on fish also decline in number.

5 Fish and shellfish are also victimized by oil spills. Many are immediately poisoned by the oil and die. Others live, but their flesh can be toxic because it is inundated with hydrocarbons. When animals eat these fish, they can become poisoned. Oil can also sink to the seabed and kill salmon eggs, crab larvae, and other eggs and larvae.

6 The oil contaminates the land's food chain. Predators such as bald eagles scavenge the bodies of dead, oily fish and bring them back to their nests to feed their young. Young eagles—and adult eagles—are then killed by eating the oiled fish. Bears eat dead, oiled fish that have washed ashore and are endangered by the spill as well. Migrating seabirds such as ducks, loons, and geese ingest oil because they nest on rocks and mudflats, eating worms and other organisms that have been contaminated with oil. Deer who come to the beach to eat kelp ingest oil as well.

3 Sea mammals are also early victims of an oil spill; sea otters are especially vulnerable. Unlike many other sea mammals, sea otters don't have a protective coating of blubber, and so depend upon their fur to insulate them from the cold. Their fur traps air, which acts as a blanket. Oil doesn't allow the fur to trap air, cutting down the insulating ability of the fur by some 70%, so otters freeze to death. Some are also killed by oil poisoning when they ingest oil while cleaning their fur or inhaling the petroleum fumes. Several thousand sea otters were killed in the massive *Exxon Valdez* spill.

7 On rocky beaches exposed to the ocean where there are large waves, the oil may be washed away within a year. On protected, sandy beaches with fewer waves, the oil remains for many years, and may become mixed with sand and buried in the soil.

How an Oil Spill Is Cleaned Up

When oil leaks out of the side of a tanker, an attempt is made to contain the spill. Floating containment booms that consist partly of buoyant foam are designed for this purpose. A flexible skirt below water level stops some of the oil from escaping beneath the boom.

Skimmers—boats specially adapted for cleaning oil spills—scoop oil from the water. There are several methods of using skimmers. The method shown here involves using an absorbent conveyor belt that constantly runs from the water to the boat, drawing oil on board. On the boat, rollers squeeze the oil from the conveyor belt. When enough oil is collected on a skimmer, the oil is loaded onto a barge and carted away.

Chemical dispersant can be added to the oil to break up the large, thick slick into small droplets. Another chemical that may help clean oil spills is *Elastol*, a powder that, when added to oil, makes it easier to skim.

Seabirds, sea otters, and other animals that have been coated with oil will die quickly from hypothermia, especially in cold water, unless they are treated. Oil is cleaned off the animals, sometimes with toothbrushes and dishwashing liquid. Sometimes animals in danger of dying are airlifted to emergency treatment centers. And wildlife experts sometimes attempt to scare animals away from the spill area by shooting off cannons and erecting scarecrows.

In some spills, such as the infamous disaster caused by the *Exxon Valdez*, the oil becomes thick and turns into mousse. When this happens, the oil may become too viscous to be picked up by skimmers. Machines known as *supersuckers*, which are essentially huge vacuum cleaners, can be used to suck off the oil. One of the most effective ways of cleaning this kind of spill is decidedly low-tech, however: Fishermen in skiffs scoop up the oil in buckets.

Oiled beaches are cleaned by high-pressure hoses and hot or cold water to wash the oil toward V-shaped booms, where the oil is collected and carted away. People also scoop up crude oil and tarballs by hand from the beach.

Bioremediation is a technique that shows promise for cleaning oil off beaches. It uses naturally occurring bacteria to break down the oil. A chemical "fertilizer" is sprayed onto oil-drenched beaches. This "fertilizer" promotes the growth of microorganisms that literally eat the oil.

CHAPTER
19

The Golden Coastal Ecosystem

THE RICHEST SOURCE of ocean life can be found along the coasts. A remarkable abundance of life exists in these shallow, nutrient-rich waters. The rest of the ocean is a biological desert when compared with the coasts.

Marine life is richest along the coasts because of the wealth of nutrients that are found here. They are washed into the ocean from wetlands and from estuaries, where fresh water meets the ocean. And the nutrients are also washed up from the deeper ocean bed to the coasts through the upwelling of currents. Phytoplankton rely on these nutrients for their own sustenance and they form the first link in the ocean's food chain.

The coasts are also where many fish spend the early part of their lives, even if they live their adult lives in more open ocean. Approximately two-thirds of fish species used by humans spend the early stages of their lives in estuaries and wetlands. And an estimated 90% of all marine fish and shellfish caught comes from the third of the ocean closest to the world's coasts.

Not only do the coasts attract marine life—they also attract droves of people. The coasts do not make up a huge percentage of all land area in the world, but sizable numbers of the world's population live near the coasts. In fact, the United Nations estimates that 60% of the world's population lives near the coasts, and more than 50% of the U.S. population lives within 50 miles of the coast.

The result is massive and widespread pollution of our coasts. Sewage effluent, agricultural runoff, overdevelopment, and the dumping of toxic heavy metals all take their toll. Beaches are often unswimmable; tales of garbage and medical refuse washing ashore are all too common. *Red tide* is caused in part by water pollution and poisons shellfish and humans who eat the contaminated shellfish. Coastal pollution kills uncounted numbers of fish and entire biological communities. We are destroying our coastal environment in an indeterminate number of ways. And as we do so, we help destroy the rest of the ocean as well.

There is nothing mysterious about the solution to this problem. The first step in saving the coasts is controlling development so that even more pollution doesn't make its way into the ocean. The practice of dumping wastes directly into the ocean must stop. Finally, landborne pollution must be curbed as well, because one way or another, it usually ends up pouring into coastal waters. Unless these preventive measures are taken, the rich life that attracts people to the coasts will vanish. This grim outcome would be one of the more bitter ironies of environmental abuse.

The Ecology of Estuaries and the Coast

Estuaries—where freshwater rivers mix with the saltwater ocean—are among the richest sources of life on earth. That's because silt and decaying plant matter wash from the river into the ocean, forming a nutrient-rich "soup." That soup supports phytoplankton, which form the first link at the bottom of the ocean's food chain. Bottom-dwelling plants, seaweed, and shellfish also thrive in this nutrient-rich environment.

Because the waters near estuaries are rich in phytoplankton, many fish species inhabit these areas. Some species that live near or in estuaries can tolerate both freshwater and saltwater. For example, the flounder spawns in the salty ocean but also lives in less salty estuaries. It can even survive for a time in freshwater alone.

Sand dunes along the coast serve a number of ecological functions. They protect the land from being eroded by the sea. They also provide nesting areas for birds such as the crab plover. Cliffs also provide nesting areas for birds such as the cliff swallow.

Estuaries are rich in insects, plants, shellfish, fish, and other marine life, so they attract huge numbers of waterbirds. Every winter in estuaries in warm and temperate climates, thousands of waterfowl fly from arctic and other cold regions to feed on the rich animal and plant life.

The coasts away from estuaries have their own unique and rich ecosystems. Rocky coasts support the most life because the rocks give plants and animals shelter from the unending ocean waves, and they allow sea water to stay onshore even during low tide. Barnacles and limpets, a type of mollusk that has a low, conical shell, attach themselves to rocks so they don't get washed away; their waterproof shells lock water inside them, helping to keep their bodies moist when the tide goes out. Many plants and animals, including crabs, starfish, and sea lettuce live in tide pools. Tide pools are pools of sea water surrounded by rocks that retain water even when the tide goes out.

How a Coastal Ecosystem Is Polluted

The vast majority of ocean pollution occurs along the coasts and is land based: The pollutants are created on land and either are dumped directly into the ocean or wash into the ocean from rivers, streams, and underground aquifers.

Runoff from agriculture and lawns includes fertilizers, pesticides, and herbicides. Nitrates from fertilizers are an especially serious problem. They contain nutrients that algae can use, which may result in massive algae blooms. After these algae die, bacteria decompose them. The bacateria use up the oxygen in the water during the decomposition process. Fish are killed and entire ecosystems are seriously harmed when too much oxygen is taken from the water in this manner. Sewage similarly leads to algae blooms.

Wetlands along the coast are lost due to development, dredging, and use as garbage dumps. This has serious effects on the ocean's environment. Wetlands normally filter out pollutants, and as there are fewer wetlands, the ocean will become more polluted. Wetlands are also nurseries for many species of fish, so killing off the wetlands kills off many fish—including many species normally caught for human consumption.

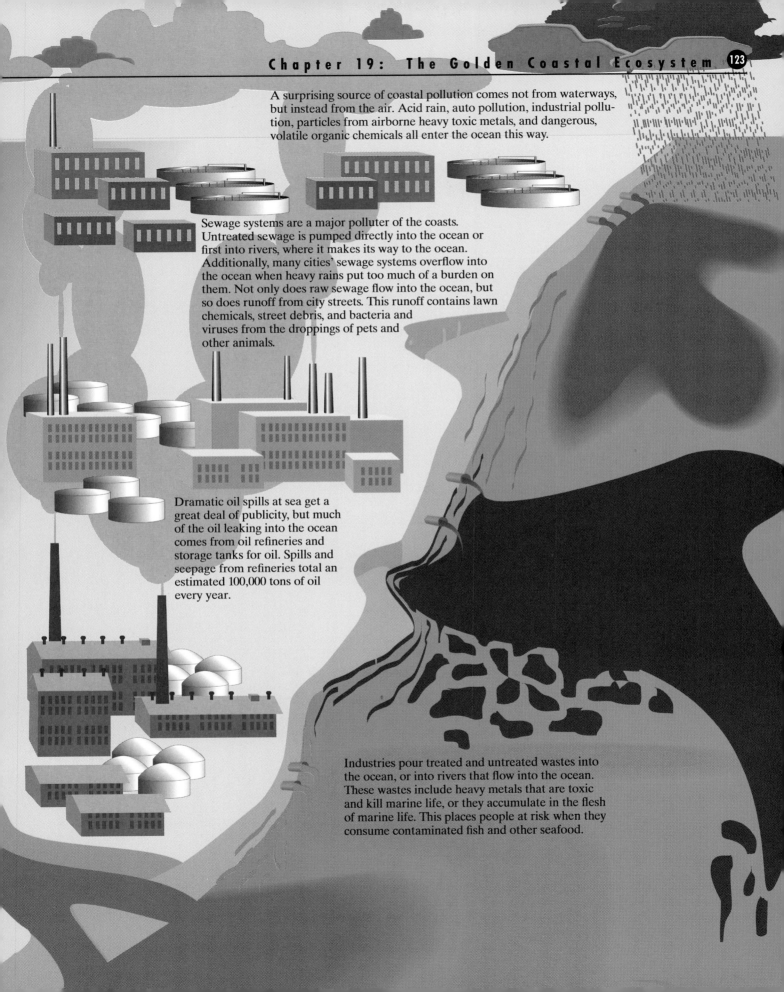

A surprising source of coastal pollution comes not from waterways, but instead from the air. Acid rain, auto pollution, industrial pollution, particles from airborne heavy toxic metals, and dangerous, volatile organic chemicals all enter the ocean this way.

Sewage systems are a major polluter of the coasts. Untreated sewage is pumped directly into the ocean or first into rivers, where it makes its way to the ocean. Additionally, many cities' sewage systems overflow into the ocean when heavy rains put too much of a burden on them. Not only does raw sewage flow into the ocean, but so does runoff from city streets. This runoff contains lawn chemicals, street debris, and bacteria and viruses from the droppings of pets and other animals.

Dramatic oil spills at sea get a great deal of publicity, but much of the oil leaking into the ocean comes from oil refineries and storage tanks for oil. Spills and seepage from refineries total an estimated 100,000 tons of oil every year.

Industries pour treated and untreated wastes into the ocean, or into rivers that flow into the ocean. These wastes include heavy metals that are toxic and kill marine life, or they accumulate in the flesh of marine life. This places people at risk when they consume contaminated fish and other seafood.

CHAPTER 20

How Coral Reefs Work

CORAL REEFS ARE some of the most peaceful and awe-inspiring spots on earth. Nurtured by warm, tropical waters, these reefs are home to some of the richest ecosystems on the planet. In fact, they are so rich that many people liken the reefs to tropical rain forests because of the remarkable variety of life they support.

Strap on a snorkel and float above a reef and you'll be faced with one of the most breathtaking experiences of your life. Hordes of brightly colored fish surround you as if you were one of their own; devilish-looking manta rays flap their waterborne wings; barracuda lurk motionless nearby. An estimated one-third of all marine species make their home in the reefs—possibly one-half million species of ocean life.

Coral reefs may be 500 million years old. This would place them among the most ancient ecosystems on earth. Reefs thrive in warm, shallow seas with temperatures ranging from 75° to 84°F. Coral generally grows within the top 65 feet of the ocean's surface, and rarely extends below 150 feet. Sunlight doesn't reach far beneath the ocean's surface, and coral can't thrive where light can't penetrate. Tiny, photosynthesizing brown algae, called *zooxanthellae,* live inside the coral and help it grow. The coral releases carbon dioxide that the zooxanthellae use during photosynthesis. In return, during photosynthesis the zooxanthellae release oxygen and carbon dioxide that the coral uses for respiration.

Coral reefs all over the world are under attack. They are mined for their limestone. Dynamite is used to break them up and they are torn apart with crowbars so that the coral can be used in building houses. Humans can destroy in a few hours what nature took several centuries to create. Oil spills and other kinds of water pollution kill reefs, as do the activities of thoughtless tourists and sport fishermen. Particularly insidious is sewage and fertilizer runoff into the ocean near reefs, because that leads to the explosive growth of the crown of thorns starfish, which eat coral at an aggressive rate: A single starfish consumes up to 55 square feet of coral a year.

Stopping pollution, coral mining, and overfishing near reefs will help save them. In some places these measures have already been taken, and the reefs there may continue to thrive. But countless other reefs are under attack, and unless we take action to protect our reefs, many of the world's most ancient and valuable ecosystems may be lost.

The Ecology of Coral Reefs

Coral reefs are so rich in marine life that they have been referred to as tropical rain forests of the ocean. They owe their existence to an intricate, symbiotic relationship between coral polyps and minute, brown photosynthesizing algae called zooxanthellae.

Tiny zooxanthellae algae live inside the coral. The coral excretes mineral wastes after eating, and carbon dioxide (CO_2) from breathing. The zooxanthellae inside the coral use the nitrogen and phosporous from the coral's wastes. During photosynthesis, the algae incorporates CO_2 from the coral into rich organic matter that sustains both the algae and the coral. The zooxanthellae also give off oxygen (O_2) during photosynthesis, which the coral uses. In this way, the coral and zooxanthellae provide each other with vital nutrients and gases that they each need in order to live. (The color of the coral is actually the color of the zooxanthellae living inside it.)

Coral reefs are created by colonies of coral polyps, marine animals related to the sea anemone that are one-tenth of an inch to several inches in size. To protect itself, each soft-bodied polyp excretes a limestone tube or cuplike structure around itself. This structure is like an external skeleton, and the polyps live inside it. Polyps usually feed at night, ingesting zooplankton that float near it, trapping the plankton in tentacles that it extends beyond the limestone structure.

Zooxanthellae

O_2

CO_2 and wastes (nutrients)

Coral

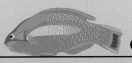
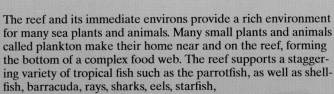

The reef and its immediate environs provide a rich environment for many sea plants and animals. Many small plants and animals called plankton make their home near and on the reef, forming the bottom of a complex food web. The reef supports a staggering variety of tropical fish such as the parrotfish, as well as shellfish, barracuda, rays, sharks, eels, starfish, urchins, sea cucumbers, and thousands of other species. A typical coral reef may have 3,000 species living on and near it.

When a coral dies, its limestone skeleton remains on the reef and hardens over time. New coral grows on top of the dead skeleton, making the reef grow even larger. Blue-green algae living on the reef excrete a calcium-containing compound, which helps bind the corals in the reef together.

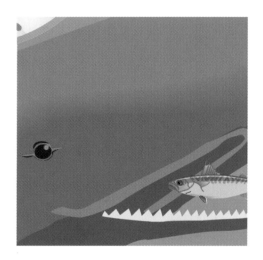

CHAPTER
21

The Endangered Whales

We account the whale immortal in his species. . . . He swam the seas before the continents broke water. . . if ever the world is to be again flooded. . . then the eternal whale will survive, and rearing upon the topmost crest of the equatorial flood, spout his frothed defiance to the skies.

—Herman Melville, *Moby Dick*

WHEN HERMAN MELVILLE wrote these words nearly 150 years ago, the whale did indeed seem immortal. The ocean was thick with these majestic creatures and their quantity and variety seemed infinite. Their illusion of immortality was gradually shattered as people started hunting whales for their blubber, oil, ivory, meat, and even bones. Many tens of thousands of the leviathans were slaughtered every year to provide products as diverse as fuel oil, cosmetics, and whalebone corsets. In the United States alone, some 70,000 people worked in the thriving whaling industry, which produced nearly 17 million gallons of whale oil and more than 5.5 million pounds of whalebones in a single year.

The slaughter took its toll. First the slow-moving and easily caught right whale became scarce, and then the humpback, gray, bowhead, sperm, blue, fin, and sei whales began to disappear. Whales nearly vanished from the Pacific and North Atlantic oceans, as well as waters around Norway, Iceland, the Shetlands, and Ireland. By the 1960s, all these species had all but disappeared.

Public pressure instigated global action to protect whales as an endangered species. As a result, the International Whaling Commission declared a worldwide ban on whaling in 1986. In 1994, a whale sanctuary was established in the Antarctic Ocean, and the hunting of whales—even for research purposes—was banned there. However, not all countries have complied with the ban through the years. Russia, Japan, Iceland, and Norway have all continued whaling intermittently since then, and Norway continues the practice today. Still, the ban has helped: In 1994, the California gray whale was plentiful enough so that it was no longer listed officially as "endangered."

Despite Norway's actions, whaling is no longer the greatest threat to the whale. Other human activities, most notably the pollution and destruction of the whale's habitat, are the main culprits.

The majority of whales die because the ocean that has been their home for millions of years has become increasingly polluted. Toxic wastes and pollution kill some outright, either by poisoning or by causing serious diseases. Noise pollution drives them from their calving grounds. We destroy the food web upon which they live when we overfish the ocean, leaving less fish, squid, and krill for whales to eat. Some whales are also killed inadvertently every year in fishing nets or in collisions with boats.

Stricter enforcement of the worldwide whaling ban is only one measure that should be taken to prevent the extinction of the whale. Many countries, such as Norway and Japan, have tried to see the ban overturned. But the approach to the problem of protecting the whales that would ultimately be most effective is to reduce ocean pollution. Since the imposition of the ban on hunting, the whale's primary enemy is not the harpoon—it's industrial, municipal, agricultural, and ocean wastes.

Dangers Facing the Whales

Many species of the world's most majestic creatures, the whales, are endangered. This species includes the largest creature that has ever lived on the planet — the blue whale, which can reach 100 feet long and weigh 175 tons. In years past, the hunting of whales killed off vast numbers of their populations, but today it is pollution and the destruction of the whale's habitat that does these amazing creatures the most harm.

Over the last century and a half, whaling has put many species of whales in danger. Whales were prized for their meat and blubber, for their oil for lamps, paint, and cosmetics, for their ivory, and even for their bones, which were used in whalebone corsets to give Victorian women hourglass-shaped figures. Mass whale killing began in the mid-1800s, with the advent of steam-powered ships and harpoons fired by cannons. In 1931, over 29,000 blue whales were killed in a single summer in Antarctica—far more blue whales than are now alive on the entire planet. In 1986 an international treaty outlawed whaling, but as of this writing, Norway does not abide by the treaty and permits commercial whaling.

Whales use their voices to communicate and navigate. Some scientists believe that before the advent of propeller ships, they could hear each other as far as thousands of miles away. Today, noise pollution in the ocean causes problems for whales. Noise from motorboats, freighters, cruise ships, supertankers, and even parasail boats and jet skis interferes with whale communications. There is some evidence that such noise pollution has been chasing whales away from the places where they normally calve.

One of the major threats to whales is the destruction of their food supply. Baleen whales are a type of whale that includes some of the larger species, such as the blue whale and right whale. Baleen whales feed on small shrimp-like creatures called krill and upon tiny plants and animals called plankton. Fishing fleets, especially the Japanese and the Russians, harvest massive quantities of krill around Antarctica, potentially depriving whales of their food supply. Some scientists believe that the depletion of the ozone layer allows an increased amount of ultraviolet rays to kill off large numbers of the phytoplankton upon which whales and krill depend.

Today, the accidental killing of whales is responsible for far more whale deaths than is commercial whaling. Some whales are caught in fishermen's nets and die there. Other whales collide with boats and are maimed and killed by the encounter. The New England Aquarium estimates that one out of every five whales that wash ashore in New England has been killed by collision with a boat.

Pollution is directly and indirectly responsible for many whale deaths. Because whales have a great deal of fatty tissue, certain toxic chemicals such as PCBs build up in their blubber. PCBs (polychlorinated biphenyls) are used by various industries. These chemicals can kill the whales directly by causing diseases such as liver cancer, and indirectly by harming their immune system and lowering their ability to fight off infections. Pollution also plays a role in the formation of blooms of *red tide*, a poisonous algae, which is eaten by fish. These poisoned fish are then eaten by whales, who can die from the toxins.

PCBs

5

FRESHWATER: THE STREAM OF LIFE

CONTENTS

WITHOUT FRESHWATER, there is no life. In fact, we are more dependent on water than on food. We get freshwater as part of the vast water cycle in which water evaporates from the ocean, falls as rain over land and gathers in lakes, rivers, streams, marshes, and other wetlands. It then returns to the ocean to begin the cycle all over again.

There seems to be vast amounts of freshwater on earth, but in fact, most of earth's water is salty. Only 2.6% of the water on earth is fresh, and of that, over 99% is locked up in glaciers, ice, and snow in the polar regions, or else it is found underground. Of the remaining 1%, almost half is found as water vapor and soil moisture, or else it is locked in the bodies of plants and animals. The final half percent or so is what we see in our lakes, streams, marshes, and rivers. In some parts of the world, this freshwater seems a boundless resource, but in other parts, it is scarce indeed.

Freshwater resources serve many vital functions. They harbor complex ecosystems of plants and animals. They are a vital link in the life cycles of species that spend part of their lives on land and other parts in water. Some marine animals are anadromous, which means they spend part of their lives in freshwater and other parts in the ocean. For example, the Atlantic salmon spends its youth in clean, fast-running oxygen-rich freshwater streams and its adult life in the ocean, returning to the streams of its birth to lay eggs.

Water is vital to life in part because it is an excellent solvent, meaning that it has the ability to dissolve sizable quantities of other substances within it. This means that water is excellent for transporting nutrients throughout the bodies of plants and animals. But this same property also makes it vulnerable to pollution—water does an excellent job of carrying pollutants throughout the environment.

We have long viewed freshwater not as a reserve that needs special care, but instead as a boundless resource that will never run dry, and as an especially efficient dump. Industries and mining companies have long seen streams and rivers as perfect ways of carrying away their wastes. Cities and other developed areas have done likewise. Farming harms waterways when animal wastes, pesticides, fertilizers, and other agricultural chemicals wash into them. And even air pollution damages freshwater: Acid rain has been killing off our lakes, especially in the Northeast.

We not only pollute freshwater—we overuse it as well. Agriculture, especially in California and other areas in the West, uses vast amounts of water, which has led to the damming of rivers, essentially destroying them as living resources—some once-mighty rivers have become little more than a series of placid lakes separated by dams. As individuals we overuse water as well, whenever we take large baths or long showers, or overwater our lawns. Civilization's unending hunger for freshwater means there is less of it to go around.

In many instances we destroy freshwater resources outright in order to develop land. Marshes and swampland are destroyed at an alarming pace in order to build shopping malls and housing developments.

The freshwater we see around us is really only in a temporary state, passing through the environment as part of the earth's vast water cycle. We should consider ourselves the custodians of freshwater, who protect this vital resource while it is within our care.

CHAPTER 22

The Ecology of Wetlands

SWAMPS. MARSHES. BOGS. The words we use to describe freshwater wetlands carry the connotation of wastelands, of areas that lack intrinsic value, and should therefore be put to productive use. In the United States this sentiment is bolstered by a long history of ridding ourselves of what we perceive as nuisances. For example, as far back as 1764, the Virginia Assembly had 40,000 acres of the Great Dismal Swamp drained so that the trees within it could be harvested for lumber. In 1994, the U.S. Fish and Wildlife Service estimates that we have destroyed more than 100 million acres of wetlands—over 50% of all the wetlands in the country.

There are three types of freshwater wetlands. *Swamps* are wet for some portions of the year and dry for others. They frequently contain trees such as bald cypresses, tupelo gums, oaks, alders, and willows. When the swamp is wet, these trees are often dormant. *Marshes* are wet year-round, and usually do not have trees growing in them but instead contain grasses, cattails, bulrushes, waterlilies, and similar plants. *Bogs* usually are not covered by water, or else have only shallow water visible, but their ground is spongy, moist, and saturated with water. The ground is made of a mat of plants called sphagnum moss that can be harvested as peat. Peat can be used as fertilizer or burned as fuel.

Wetlands provide vital ecological resources for wildlife and the environment. They are prime breeding areas for many varieties of fish, shellfish, amphibians, waterfowl, mammals, and innumerable other animals. Wetlands serve as habitats for many of these animals as well as many plants. Many songbirds and waterfowl could not live without wetlands.

However, wetlands are much more than nurseries and habitats. They can also store enormous amounts of water, which prevents flooding and also keeps the water table high in times of drought. They even act as natural water purifiers by filtering out pollutants.

Wetlands are destroyed when they are filled in and developed, and when they are used for agriculture. In recent years, various wetland protection acts have gone into effect to protect these once-maligned environments. But these laws are not enough. Wetlands such as the Everglades are still under attack. Until there is widespread recognition of their important environmental role, such attacks will continue.

The Ecology of a Marsh

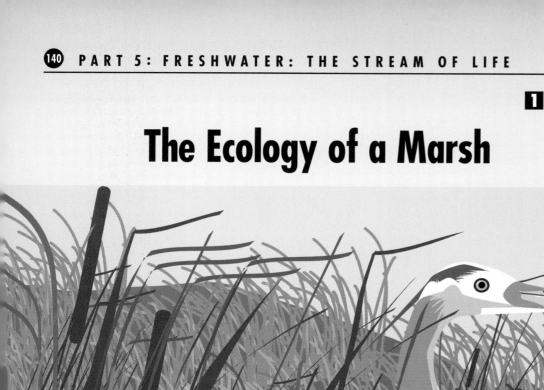

1 Wetlands, which include marshes, bogs, and swamps, are formed in several different ways, but they all have one common factor: The water table is at or near the surface of the land where they form. The *water table* is the upper limit of land that is completely saturated with water. Marshes are often created when plants such as reeds and bulrushes grow along the edge of an existing pond, lake, or inlet. These plants slow the drainage of the water and trap silt.

4 The vegetation provides both food and shelter for the marsh's animal life. Many insects spend the first part of their lives as larvae in the water, where they feed on live and rotting vegetation. They in turn are fed upon by fish and amphibians. Small birds, fish, and amphibians such as frogs and newts feed on insects. Birds such as herons feed on fish and amphibians. And reeds and rushes provide nesting grounds for waterfowl such as the moorhen.

2 As the plants slow the flow of water and trap silt, more plants are able to grow even farther from the edge of shore. These new plants trap more silt and slow the flow of water further, allowing even more plants to grow until all or most of the pond, lake, or inlet becomes overgrown and forms a marsh.

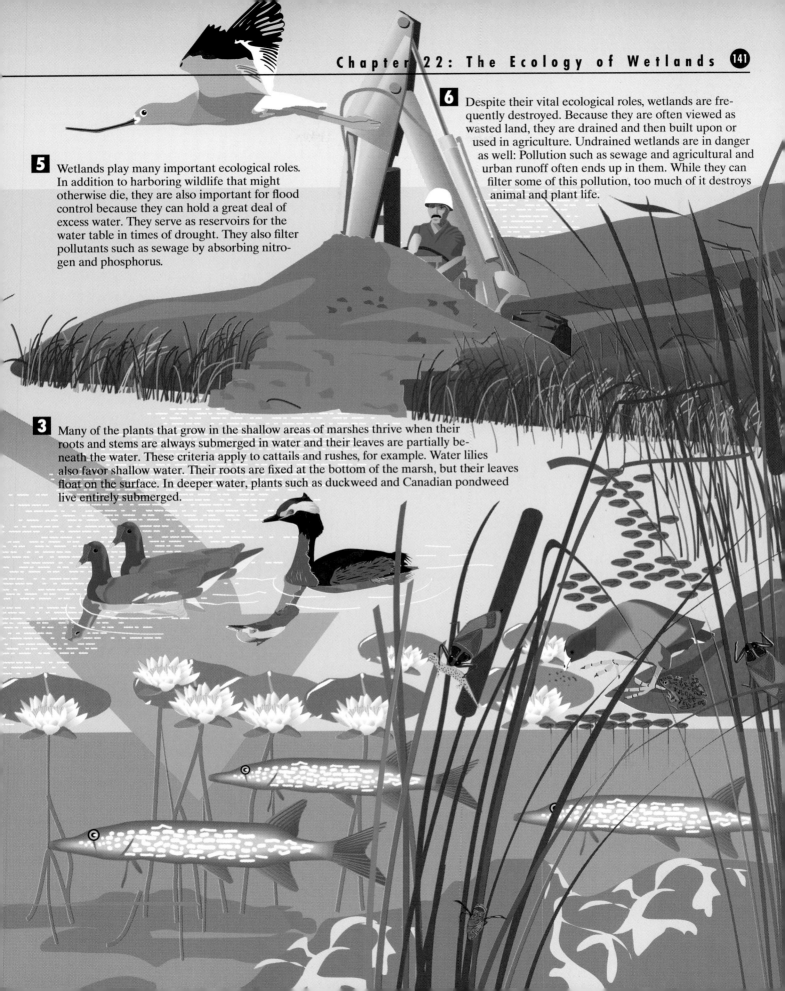

5 Wetlands play many important ecological roles. In addition to harboring wildlife that might otherwise die, they are also important for flood control because they can hold a great deal of excess water. They serve as reservoirs for the water table in times of drought. They also filter pollutants such as sewage by absorbing nitrogen and phosphorus.

6 Despite their vital ecological roles, wetlands are frequently destroyed. Because they are often viewed as wasted land, they are drained and then built upon or used in agriculture. Undrained wetlands are in danger as well: Pollution such as sewage and agricultural and urban runoff often ends up in them. While they can filter some of this pollution, too much of it destroys animal and plant life.

3 Many of the plants that grow in the shallow areas of marshes thrive when their roots and stems are always submerged in water and their leaves are partially beneath the water. These criteria apply to cattails and rushes, for example. Water lilies also favor shallow water. Their roots are fixed at the bottom of the marsh, but their leaves float on the surface. In deeper water, plants such as duckweed and Canadian pondweed live entirely submerged.

The Anatomy of a Lake

LAKES AND PONDS may seem placid and unmoving, but often they are teeming with life. The ponds and lakes are constantly undergoing a life cycle of youth, maturity, and eventual death. These bodies of water may have formed when they were gouged out of the earth by glaciers, when shifts in the earth created basins, when beavers or humans built dams for a stream or river, or when a river changed course, creating what is known as an ox-bow lake.

Within lakes and ponds is a complex ecosystem that in some ways mirrors the more vast ecosystem of the ocean. Algae on the surface of lakes and ponds grow by using energy from sunlight and nutrients from the lake. These algae are eaten by zooplankton, which are in turn eaten by progressively larger animals in a complex food web. When lake plants and animals die and decompose, the resulting particles fall to the bottom of the lake, where they are broken down by microorganisms. That broken-down material is used by algae as nutrients, beginning the cycle all over again.

Lakes consist of several zones. Nearest to the shore is the *littoral zone*, where cattails, grasslike vegetation, amphibians, waterfowl, and many other plants and animals live. The open water in the middle of the lake is called the *pelagic zone*. The depth of water to which sunlight can penetrate the surface of the water is called the *limnetic zone*, and it is here that algae live. Beneath the limnetic zone is the *benthic zone*, or *profundal zone* in very deep lakes such as the Great Lakes. This is the deepest zone, and it is here that many fish live. At the very bottom of lakes are areas of mud and silt filled with microorganisms that break down organic matter. There is little oxygen at the lake bottom, so many of these microbes are *anaerobic*, meaning that they do not need oxygen to live. Some older lakes fill with silt and become rich with nutrients. This leads to greater algae growth, and more rooted plants growing in the lake. Eventually, the lake fills in with vegetation and silt and becomes a marsh.

Lakes are endangered in many ways. Acid rain and pollution kill plant and animal life in them. Sewage and agricultural runoff lead to *eutrophication*, in which oxygen in the water is depleted. We take more water out of some lakes for water supplies than is replaced by rain and streams, and these lakes shrink or eventually dry up. Lakes are not a permanent resource, and they need protection like other resources do. Unless we treat them with care, some lakes may vanish forever.

Anatomy of a Lake

1 A lake's food web, like the ocean's, begins with phytoplankton, tiny plants that convert sunlight and nutrients into living matter. In lakes, these are mainly single-celled green or blue-green algae that thrive in the open water in the middle of the lake, called the pelagic zone. The layer of water to which light can penetrate is called the limnetic zone. Algae can also be found here, as well as higher forms of life.

2 Zooplankton such as the cyclops feed upon algae. Zooplankton are in turn fed upon by small fish, and these small fish are fed upon by larger fish, which are fed upon by birds, large amphibians, and mammals.

3 Below the limnetic zone is an area called the benthic zone; in very deep lakes such as the Great Lakes, it is called the profundal zone. Fish such as trout, perch, bass, and pickerel live here, feeding on insect larvae and detritus, or particles from decomposing plants and animals, that fall to the benthic zone from the limnetic zone.

6 Cold water is denser than warm water, so warm water floats upon cold water. During the summer, the warm water forms the top layer of the lake. During the fall, the water on top of the lake cools and the water at the bottom is warmer. In this case, water from the bottom of the lake flows to the top and water from the top flows to the bottom. This process brings nutrients up from the bottom of the lake, feeding algae at the top. It also brings the oxygen-rich water from the top to the oxygen-poor lake bottom. In the spring, the topmost water warms and the layers of water are again reversed.

Littoral zone

Pelagic zone

Limnetic zone

Benthic zone

4 The littoral zone, that shallow area of a lake closest to shore, is home to vegetation such as cattails, reeds, water lilies, and submerged plants. These plants provide food and shelter for other forms of life such as insect larvae, adult insects, frogs, snakes, snails, fish, and birds. Underwater plants provide cover for crayfish. Insects and their larvae feed upon plants, and frogs and snakes feed upon insects.

5 Organic debris from dead plants, animals, and algae falls to the bottom of the lake, into mud and silt. The dead plant and animal matter is decomposed at the bottom by bacteria. Some bacterial decomposition uses up oxygen. If there is too much decomposing matter, oxygen is depleted, leaving little oxygen in the lake for the plants and animals.

The Ecology of Rivers

I N THEIR NATURAL state, rivers support a remarkable amount and variety of wildlife. Fish, crustaceans, plants, birds, frogs, turtles, crocodiles, bears, deer—the teeming plant and animal life in a river and along a river's banks is remarkable. The variety of life along a river changes according to its proximity to the river's source. The river's source, often high in the mountains, is fed by ice, snow and glaciers, rain, and lakes or springs. The river here is often shallow and fast moving, streaming over rocks, and heavily oxygenated. There is not much wildlife or plant life living in the river at its source—plankton don't thrive in fast-moving water, so they cannot form the bottom of a food web. Instead, nutrients wash into the river from its banks, feeding insect larvae and fish that live upon the larvae.

As the river moves downstream it becomes slower and richer in nutrients, plant life, and animal life. Here is where most of the life of the river can be found.

Life no longer teems in many of our rivers, because so many of the great rivers in the United States are endangered. We use rivers as dumps for industrial, agricultural, urban, and suburban waste. We dam them to provide drinking water and water for industry and agriculture, and to generate electricity. Nothing symbolizes the plight of rivers more than the Cuyahoga River in the Great Lakes region, which caught fire in 1969 because it was so inundated with pollutants.

Other rivers on the endangered list include the Penobscot in Maine, the Mississippi in the great heartland, the Colorado in the West, and the Columbia and Snake Rivers in the Pacific Northwest. The Columbia River once gushed and teemed with more than 15 million salmon a year in fish runs, but today it is little more than a series of languid lakes because of the 16 dams that have pacified this once-proud river.

The first step toward saving these and other rivers is to stop polluting them. Unchecked development must be halted as well. And water conservation measures must be put into effect—as well as a curb on our insatiable demand for electricity.

The Ecology of a River

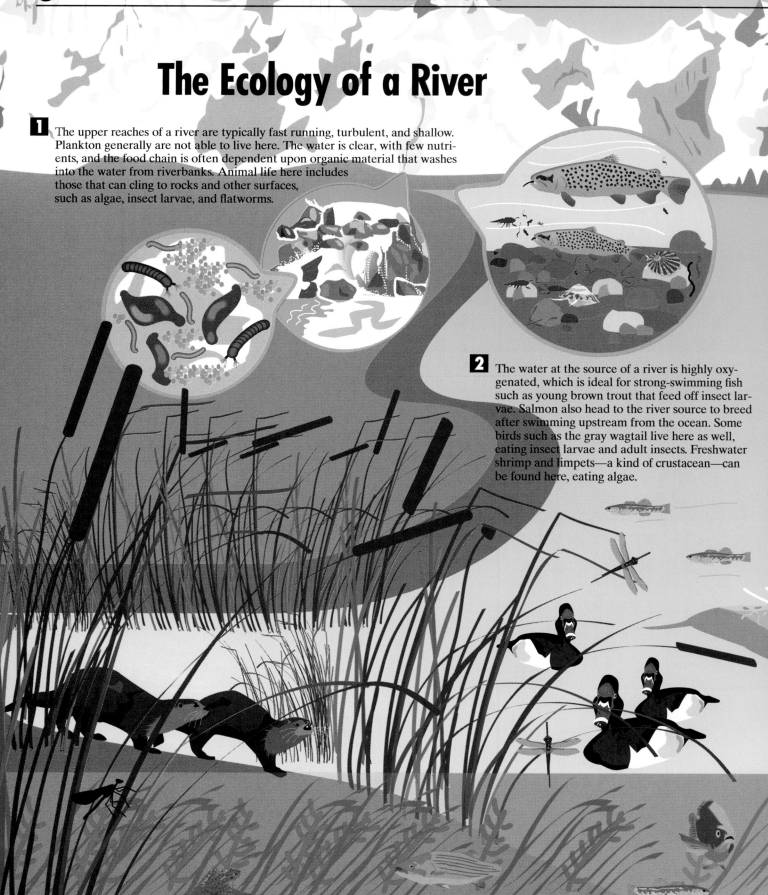

1 The upper reaches of a river are typically fast running, turbulent, and shallow. Plankton generally are not able to live here. The water is clear, with few nutrients, and the food chain is often dependent upon organic material that washes into the water from riverbanks. Animal life here includes those that can cling to rocks and other surfaces, such as algae, insect larvae, and flatworms.

2 The water at the source of a river is highly oxygenated, which is ideal for strong-swimming fish such as young brown trout that feed off insect larvae. Salmon also head to the river source to breed after swimming upstream from the ocean. Some birds such as the gray wagtail live here as well, eating insect larvae and adult insects. Freshwater shrimp and limpets—a kind of crustacean—can be found here, eating algae.

3 As the river makes its way toward the ocean it widens, deepens, and slows. The kinds of plants and animals that live in this part of the river are different than those that live in the fast-running upper regions. Since the water is slower moving, plants can put down roots. These plants provide food and shelter for a wide variety of wildlife, especially along the riverbank, including fish, waterfowl, and mammals such as otters.

4 In addition to widening, deepening, and slowing as it flows, the river also becomes richer in nutrients and small invertebrates. The nutrients are washed into the water from riverbanks. The invertebrates, including snails, worms, and insect larvae, are carried along by the current. Also present are many floating plants. All these provide food sources for other invertebrates and fish such as the bream, which in turn are eaten by predators such as turtles, birds, and crocodiles.

5 The lowest parts of rivers are warm, sluggish, and extremely rich in nutrients and silt, which have washed into it for the entire length of the river. Because the water flows so slowly and is so filled with sediment and nutrients, it tends to be muddy looking, so fish and other water life have a difficult time seeing where they are going. Some water animals have developed specialized means of getting around this sometimes lightless environment. The river dolphin, for example, navigates by means of *sonar*—bouncing sound waves off of objects to locate them. And the electric eel uses electricity instead of its other sense organs to find its prey.

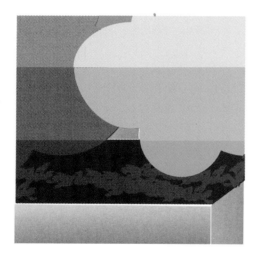

CHAPTER

25

How Sewage Treatment Works

WHERE THERE IS civilization there is sewage; we cannot escape it. Civilizations have always developed sewage systems for disposing of wastes. In fact, sewers have been unearthed in the ruins of many ancient civilizations, including the Assyrians, the Babylonians, and the ancient Greeks. The Romans erected storm-water sewers that are still being used today. In the Middle Ages cesspools were built in Europe. When cesspools were cleaned, the waste was either dumped into streams and land or used as fertilizer.

By the twentieth century, thousands of miles of sewage lines were removing human waste from cities and towns. The problem was that sewage was often left untreated and was dumped into rivers, streams, and oceans. The health and environmental effects of this are manifold. Diseases spread. Toxic wastes kill plant and animal life. And the nutrients in the waste kill off waterways by encouraging the supergrowth of algae: When the algae die, all the oxygen in the water is used up by the bacteria that break them down. This process is called *eutrophication*—the addition of excessive, abnormal amounts of nutrients—and leads to the death of plant and animal life from lack of oxygen.

Sewage treatment plants use a combination of filtering, and chemical and biological technologies to clean sewage and wastewater. Some of the most modern plants are so efficient that sewage is turned into clean fertilizer that farmers and gardeners can use, and the cleaned water can be used in nonfood farming.

Even the best sewage treatment plants, though, cannot completely solve the sewage problem. The lines leading into them are often outdated and combine the sewage from storm sewers and wastewater sewers. Storm sewers carry away runoff from storms and heavy rains, while wastewater sewers carry off human waste. If these sewer lines are combined, in times of heavy rains sewage treatment plants cannot handle all the water brought to them by storm drains, so the water is discharged into waterways without being treated—including untreated human wastes, not just storm runoff.

This is one case in which the solution is clear. It doesn't pit environmentalists against business interests, and it doesn't require massive changes in the way people live or think about the environment. It requires a different kind of green solution: the application of dollar bills. Spend enough money to build the most modern treatment plants and sewage systems, and most of the problems will be solved.

How a Sewage Treatment Plant Works

Sewage is treated in three stages. Many treatment plants employ only the first one or two of the three stages shown here. In the primary stage of treatment, large objects, nonbiodegradable objects and 60% of the solids that are suspended in the sewage, 30% of organic matter, and up to 15% of nutrients are removed from sewage, mainly through mechanical methods.

Primary Treatment

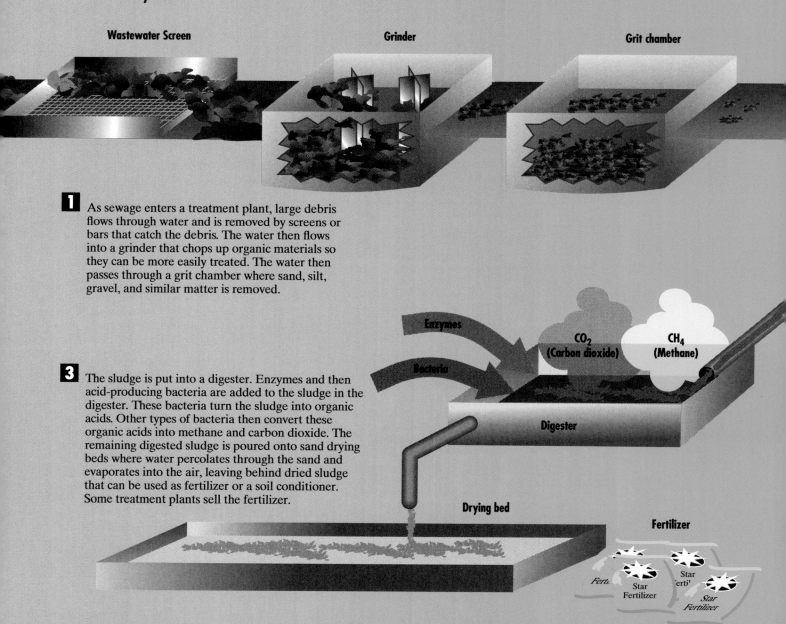

Wastewater Screen

Grinder

Grit chamber

1 As sewage enters a treatment plant, large debris flows through water and is removed by screens or bars that catch the debris. The water then flows into a grinder that chops up organic materials so they can be more easily treated. The water then passes through a grit chamber where sand, silt, gravel, and similar matter is removed.

3 The sludge is put into a digester. Enzymes and then acid-producing bacteria are added to the sludge in the digester. These bacteria turn the sludge into organic acids. Other types of bacteria then convert these organic acids into methane and carbon dioxide. The remaining digested sludge is poured onto sand drying beds where water percolates through the sand and evaporates into the air, leaving behind dried sludge that can be used as fertilizer or a soil conditioner. Some treatment plants sell the fertilizer.

Enzymes

Bacteria

CO_2 (Carbon dioxide)

CH_4 (Methane)

Digester

Drying bed

Fertilizer

Star Fertilizer

2 Much of the organic matter in the water is removed through the next step—*sedimentation*. The water flows into a sedimentation tank, where organic materials settle to the bottom and are then disposed of. Sedimentation can be aided when chemicals such as aluminum sulfate are added to wastewater. This causes solids that are suspended in the water to attach to one another and fall to the bottom of the sedimentation tank. The solid materials that settle in a sedimentation tank are called sludge.

4 After sedimentation, wastewater receives secondary treatment. This stage removes 90% of remaining organic matter and 30% to 50% of the nutrients. Microorganisms are used to further clean wastes from the water. There are several different methods for doing this. One method uses a trickling filter to place wastewater over a bed of porous material, which has on it a film of microorganisms. The microorganisms absorb the organic matter from the wastewater and convert it to carbon dioxide and water. The cleaned water then passes through a *secondary clarifier* that takes the bacteria out of the water.

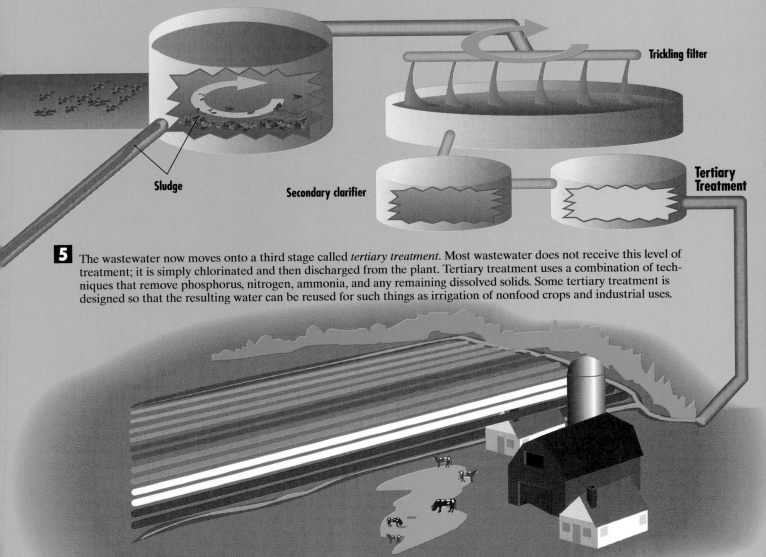

Sedimentation tank

Secondary Treatment

Trickling filter

Sludge

Secondary clarifier

Tertiary Treatment

5 The wastewater now moves onto a third stage called *tertiary treatment*. Most wastewater does not receive this level of treatment; it is simply chlorinated and then discharged from the plant. Tertiary treatment uses a combination of techniques that remove phosphorus, nitrogen, ammonia, and any remaining dissolved solids. Some tertiary treatment is designed so that the resulting water can be reused for such things as irrigation of nonfood crops and industrial uses.

THE ENERGY
CONUNDRUM

CONTENTS

NO MATTER HOW much energy we use, we always want more. Most of the countries of the industrialized world are energy gluttons. To makes things even worse, we also waste a lot of this energy. The industrialized world is responsible for most, but not all, of our energy-created environmental problems. Deserts result when wood is cut down for fuel in nonindustrialized nations, for example. And rain forests are also cut down for fuel, causing significant environmental problems.

Energy consumption is at the root of most environmental problems. Global warming is due in large part to the increasing amount of carbon dioxide in our atmosphere—and that excess carbon dioxide is created by automobile exhaust and the burning of coal and oil by industry and electric generation plants. Smog is caused by automobile exhaust; acid rain by the burning of coal in factories and electric plants. Oil spills are caused because we need to move oil from place to place. Rivers are dammed and destroyed, in large part so that large hydroelectric plants can be constructed. The list could go on and on. Unchecked energy consumption may be the largest environmental problem we face.

Nuclear energy is probably the most controversial energy source. Some people believe that nuclear energy doesn't extract the environmental toll that fossil fuels do, but many others point to radiation's cancer-causing abilities and the fact that there is no way to safely dispose of nuclear byproducts, and say that nuclear power is a dangerous source of energy.

However, not all energy sources are dangerous. Alternative energy sources do not cause environmental problems as does the burning of fossil fuels. Unlike fossil fuels, these sources never dry up. Unlike nuclear energy, they do not cause health problems, and they have few dangerous byproducts associated with them. These energy sources tap the energy of the sun either directly or indirectly. In the case of solar power, the sun's energy is used either to heat houses and water, or else to generate electricity. With wind energy, windmills called wind turbines generate electricity—and wind is created by the sun, so that wind energy is really just another form of solar energy. Unfortunately, though, we do not rely on those alternative sources—we use an insignificant amount of energy created by them.

We use energy to create electricity, to transport us, to power industry, and to use in our homes. Some 37% of all energy used in the United States goes to generate electricity. This is where coal is often used: 57% of all electricity in the United States in 1992 was generated by the burning of coal. Nuclear energy accounted for 20% of all electricity generated. Alternative energy sources, including geothermal power, created only 0.4% of our electricity.

Twenty-seven percent of all the energy used was for gasoline. The amount of gasoline we use is inconceivably large: Some 2.6 trillion gallons of unleaded gasoline were used in our country in 1990, with many deleterious effects. But oil products such as gasoline cause more problems than just the obvious ones you see spewing out of car exhausts. Virtually every phase of using oil causes pollution, from extracting it from the ground to transporting it, storing it, refining it, and burning it. For example, the Environmental Protection Agency (EPA) says that in 1992 alone, more than 2 million tons of pollutants were emitted by United States oil refineries.

In this section we'll examine various aspects of how energy affects the environment. We'll look at the problems caused by oil, coal, and natural gas, the so-called "fossil fuels." Coal and oil are the primary culprits in environmental destruction wrought by energy consumption. We'll also see how over millions of years coal, oil, and gas are created.

Solutions to the energy conundrum are relatively simple: We must consume less energy, and we must use energy sources that are nonpolluting and sustainable. The problem, at this point, isn't really technological: It's economic and political. When energy is used, the financial impact of its environmental effects aren't taken into account. For example, when coal-burning plants generate electricity, the costly environmental effects of that burning are not borne by the owners of the plant. States hundreds or even thousands of miles away pay the price when acid rain destroys their lakes—and those states, not the electric plant, have to pay for the cleanup. Long-term costs associated with energy production aren't taken into account when energy is used. Therefore, on the surface, burning coal and oil appears less costly than building windmills or using solar energy. If alternative energy sources were given financial incentives, and if there were similar conservation incentives, we would go a long way toward controlling our reliance on energy.

If we are more conscious of habits that are wasteful or harmful to the environment, we are in a better position to reform. Individual actions, no matter how small, can also help solve the problem. Every time we drive a car instead of walk, bike, or use public transportation, we reinforce our dependence on energy. When we turn our air conditioners to "high," or turn up our heaters a degree or two, we contribute to the problem.

CHAPTER
26

Our Fossil Legacy: Oil, Coal, and Natural Gas

OUR WORLD RUNS on fossil fuels: coal, natural gas, and oil. Fossil fuels were formed when plants died many millions of years ago, and through biological and chemical reactions, heat, and pressure over time, they were transformed into coal, oil, and natural gas. We use fossil fuels to power our cars, trucks, airplanes, and factories. They heat our homes. They provide electricity for our lights and washing machines and microwave ovens.

Our dependence on coal, natural gas, and oil is costly. A remarkable number of our environmental problems are created by an overreliance on coal and oil—they foul everything from the ocean to fresh water to the land to the sky itself. The burning of coal is a primary cause of acid rain. The burning of coal and oil results in air pollution. Global warming is due in part to how much fossil fuel we burn. The mining of coal destroys the land and pollutes rivers and streams. The storage, extraction, and transportation of oil pollutes the ocean, fresh water, and land. It is safe to say that coal and oil together probably wreak more environmental devastation than any other single cause on the planet. By comparison, our use of natural gas is relatively benign.

Numbers can tell the story of how addicted we are to fossil fuels. In 1992, these three sources provided some 80.4% of all the commercial energy consumed in the United States—36.7% provided by oil and its derivatives, 22.6% by natural gas, and 21.1% by coal.

Fossil fuels are a nonrenewable resource. This means that once they're used up, they're gone forever, and we are running out of them. It takes nature several hundred million years to create these fuels. We burn them in an instant.

One way for us to wean ourselves from fossil fuels is to use relatively nonpolluting, renewable sources of energy instead. These include the so-called "alternative" energy sources such as solar power and wind power. That by itself, though, is not enough; at the rate at which we currently consume energy, it is unlikely that these sources will ever be able to provide all the power we need. We must conserve energy as well. It's not only industry and governments that must do their part: We all have to work on conservation. Turning down thermostats a few degrees; biking, walking, or using public transportation instead of our automobiles whenever possible; and even driving a little slower on the highways, will all make a difference. Taken together, these little steps can mean a huge difference in energy consumption—and cleaner earth, water, and sky as well.

How Coal Is Formed

1 The coal we mine today had its beginnings hundreds of millions of years ago in prehistoric swamps—especially those of the Carboniferous period, between 345 and 280 million years ago. Lush, tropical swamps covered much of the earth then; among the vegetation were vast numbers of huge, tree-sized ferns.

Peat

2 When the vegetation died, some of it was covered by water. Because there is relatively little oxygen under water, the vegetation was slowly and only partially decomposed by bacteria. The vegetable matter lost oxygen faster than carbon. This process led to the partial decomposition of huge layers of peat in the swamps.

Lignite

3 Over millions of years, the peat was covered by layers of sand, mud, and sedimentary rocks such as sandstone, and it sank further into the earth. As the peat sank, it was heated by the earth, which becomes warmer toward its core. A combination of the pressure of the sand, mud, rocks above it, and the heat from the earth below hardened the peat and increased its carbon content. It was transformed into lignite, a soft brown coal with about 60% carbon content.

Bituminous Coal

Anthracite Coal

4 Over more millions of years, more layers of sediment and rock buried the lignite even deeper. The increased pressure and heat turned the lignite into harder bituminous coal, with 92% carbon content, and then finally into the most expensive and efficient coal, anthracite coal, with over 92% carbon content.

How Oil and Natural Gas Are Formed

1 Oil and natural gas have their origins in prehistoric oceans—mainly those in existence between 30 and 180 million years ago. Vast amounts of microscopic plants called phytoplankton sank to the bottom of the ocean and were buried along with sand and silt.

Natural Gas   Natural Gas

Oil   Oil

2 The mass of organic matter from the phytoplankton could not be completely decomposed by the bacteria because complete decomposition requires oxygen, and the ocean bottom is not rich in oxygen. The partially decomposed plant matter was buried beneath sand, sediment, and sedimentary rock. The pressure and heat over millions of years changed the partially decomposed matter into oil and natural gas.

Natural Gas

Oil

3 Over time, gas and oil flow up from deep in the earth through porous sandstone and other sedimentary rock, and move closer to the surface. When the oil and gas encounter impermeable rocks that do not allow them to flow further up, they form into vast pools of oil and gas. Typically, the gas is at the top of these pools, while the oil is at the bottom.

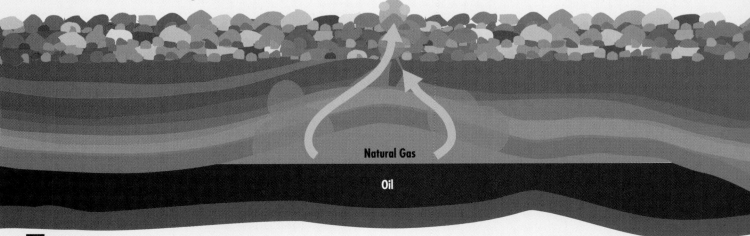

Chernobyl's Deadly Harvest: The Dangers of Nuclear Power

APRIL 26, 1986—CHERNOBYL. The very word summons a vision of hell on earth: a nuclear reaction raging out of control, spewing poisonous wastes over not only the immediate countryside but throughout Europe and the world. Massive amounts of radioctivity were released into the atmosphere—some say the equivalent of ten or more of the atomic bombs dropped on Hiroshima. Dozens of deaths occurred in the first few days. Months and years later, cancers, leukemias, and other diseases were caused by the radiation.

The main reasons for the Chernobyl disaster were poor plant design, incompetence, and poorly designed safety features. Some who favor nuclear power say that such circumstances will never conspire again. They believe that nuclear power doesn't cause the environmental damage that burning fossil fuels does.

But others say Chernobyl was an accident waiting to happen. This camp believes that more accidents are inevitable. And, they add, while Chernobyl may be the most visible symbol of the danger of nuclear power, *any* use of nuclear power is inherently dangerous and brings with it unacceptable risks.

The debate over the "peaceful" use of nuclear power has raged ever since the atom bomb was exploded over Hiroshima. In general, nuclear proponents have won. Approximately 20% of the electricity produced in the United States is generated by nuclear power plants. The other 80% comes from coal, oil, gas, hydroelectric, and alternative energy sources. Both the normal operations of nuclear plants, as well as the possibility of a nuclear catastrophe, concerns those who believe that nuclear power is inherently unsafe.

Virtually every step in the creation of nuclear power creates radioactive nuclear waste capable of causing leukemia, a variety of cancers, genetic mutations, and other health problems. Uranium is mined to produce nuclear fuel, and this type of mining exposes miners to dangerous levels of radiation. Processing the uranium into nuclear fuel releases radiation into the air and water and creates radioactive wastes. The spent fuel from nuclear power plants will remain radioactive for tens of thousands of years—and science still has not come up with a way to dispose of it safely. In fact, nuclear reactors themselves become radioactive and must be shut down after 25 to 40 years—and again, no one knows how to make the radioactive reactor safe after it has been shut down.

It may be true that future disasters like the Chernobyl accident can be averted, but no one is really sure of this. What is certain is that nuclear power creates dangerous radioactive wastes that will be with us for tens of thousands of years. Unless we curb our insatiable demand for energy or come up with cleaner, renewable sources of energy, the problem won't go away.

Chernobyl's Deadly Harvest: How the Accident Happened

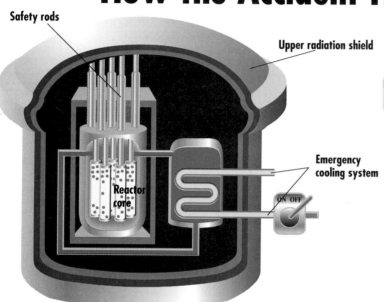

Safety rods

Upper radiation shield

Emergency cooling system

Reactor core

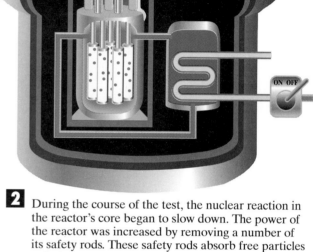

1 The Chernobyl disaster was caused when engineers at the plant ran a safety test. The flawed design of the safety test was the first big mistake: It called for turning off the emergency cooling system of the plant during the test. The emergency cooling system, a series of pipes through which cool water is pumped, kicks in when a nuclear reaction begins to overheat. The cooling system prevents the reaction from raging out of control. This emergency cooling system backs up the reactor's normal cooling system.

2 During the course of the test, the nuclear reaction in the reactor's core began to slow down. The power of the reactor was increased by removing a number of its safety rods. These safety rods absorb free particles called neutrons, which power a nuclear reaction. The rods are lowered or raised through water-filled tubes into the reactor's core. When the rods were removed, the reaction heated up and coolant started to boil out the reactor's pipes. At this point, the reactor had become dangerously unstable. Since the emergency cooling systems had been disabled, they could not cool down the reactor.

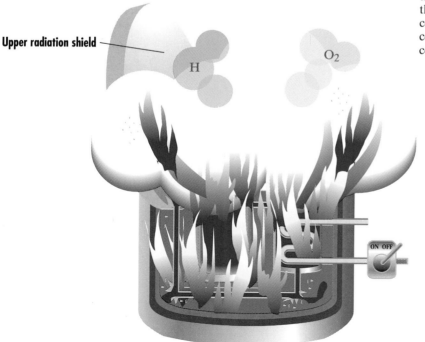

Upper radiation shield

H

O_2

4 The power surge caused steam explosions, which ripped apart pipes in the normal cooling system that all reactors have. It also caused the formation of hydrogen and oxygen gases, which accumulated inside the reactor's containment vessel. These gases then ignited in a huge explosion that knocked off a radiation shield above the reactor, blew a hole through the top of the plant and spewed 50 tons of highly radioactive material into the atmosphere. The power surge also caused raging fires throughout the plant.

3 In an attempt to slow down the reaction, the safety rods were lowered back into the reactor's core. What wasn't considered was that the first meter or so of each rod is hollow, and so cannot absorb neutrons to slow down a reaction. Only after the first meter is lowered do the rods begin to slow down the reaction. As the rods are lowered, they displace water—water that acts to slow down the reaction. So the rods being lowered simultaneously actually increased the nuclear reaction by displacing the neutron-absorbing water. This caused a huge power surge.

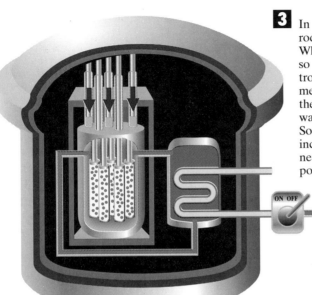

Radiation

Radiation

5 The nuclear core raged out of control and became so hot that it melted through a lower radiation shield and burned its way to the bottom of the plant. It continued to burn and spew radiation into the atmosphere. It is believed that the uncontrolled nuclear reaction in the core stopped only when the material in the core spread throughout the bowels and pipes of the bottom of the plant, dispersing so much that the reaction cooled down and stopped. This material, though, remains highly radioactive.

CHAPTER
28

Green Machines: The Promise of Alternative Energy Sources

FOSSIL FUELS AND nuclear energy are the world's two major sources of energy. Sadly, they also are responsible for much of the world's pollution. Ever since the Industrial Revolution made coal king, energy consumption has waged an attack on the environment.

It doesn't have to be that way. Energy need not pollute. Instead, it can be clean and in endless supply. Energy that is always renewing itself is called alternative energy or renewable energy.

Renewable energy sources include solar power, wind power, geothermal power, tidal power, hydroelectric power, and biomass energy—the burning of methane, wood, and other plant matter. Unfortunately, some of these energy sources can cause environmental problems; wood burning, for example, pollutes the atmosphere. And hydroelectric power, while it is renewable, also carries a heavy environmental toll—it destroys free-running rivers and the life within them.

Solar power and wind power are the most promising renewable energy sources. In fact, both of them harness the energy of the sun—solar power directly and wind power indirectly, since the wind is created by the sun's heating of the atmosphere.

Solar energy can be used in several ways. Sunlight can be directly converted to electricity by photovoltaic cells, sometimes called solar cells. Typically, many solar cells are combined in large solar arrays in order to produce sufficient amounts of electricity.

Solar energy can also heat a building and provide hot water within a building. Passive solar energy typically doesn't require any special equipment. A building that uses passive solar energy is designed so the sun will provide the maximum heat during cold weather. Active solar energy, on the other hand, requires some kind of mechanical system to harness the sun's heat, often for heating water.

Wind, one of humankind's first energy sources, was used initially to pump water for irrigation. Today, however, wind turbines run generators that produce electricity. They are sophisticated pieces of machinery that combine aerodynamic design, microprocessors, and electricity generators. Many of them are arrayed in so-called "wind farms" that can produce sizable amounts of electricity.

We know how to harness wind and solar power to produce electricity. However, renewable energy in many cases is more expensive than traditional nonrenewable sources. Until governments find ways to make alternative sources of energy less expensive, we'll continue to employ the polluting sources of energy that we use today.

How a Solar Cell Works

1 Solar cells convert sunlight into electricity. Each individual cell produces only a small amount of electricity, but when many of them are combined in a solar array, a substantial amount of electricity can be produced.

2 Solar cells basically consist of a substrate, which is at the very bottom of the cell, and two layers of silicon that rest on top of the substrate. The substrate is made of an inert material such as glass or plastic, and it holds the rest of the cell together. The lower section of silicon is called the P-type layer, and the upper section is called the N-type layer. Silicon is the same material found in microprocessors. Negative and positive terminals made out of metal are used to conduct the flow of electricity from the N-type layer to the P-type layer.

3 The N-type layer and P-type layer are made of slightly different types of silicon, and so have different properties. N-type silicon attracts negatively charged electrons, while P-type silicon attracts *holes*—atoms missing an electron. The N-type layer therefore has a negative charge, and the P-type layer has a positive charge. Because these layers have different charges, where they meet they create an electric field.

Electrons

Atom

Electron

Solar cell

N-type layer

(−) Negative terminal

Positive terminal (+)

P-type layer

Hole

Substrate

(+)

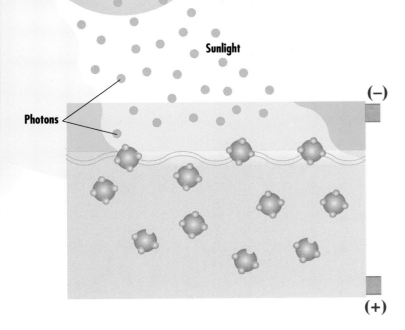

Sunlight

Photons

(−)

(+)

4 When sunlight strikes the solar cell, it travels through the N-type layer, which is usually thin and transparent, allowing for sunlight to travel through. It then strikes somewhere near the junction of the N-type layer and the P-type layer.

5 Sunlight carries energy in the form of photons, which are particles of light. When a photon hits a silicon atom, it frees an electron. If this happens near the junction of the N-type and P-type layers, the electric field found there pushes the electron toward the N-type layer, giving that layer a negative charge. It pushes the atom with the "hole" in it toward the P-type layer, giving that layer a positive charge.

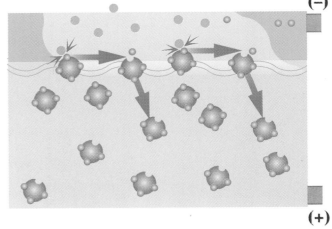

(−)

(+)

6 When a circuit is made by connecting the contact on the N-type layer to the contact on the P-type layer, electricity will flow from the negative layer to the positive layer. This is because the electrons from the negative layer are attracted to the positive layer—they rush in to fill the "holes" in the atoms there.

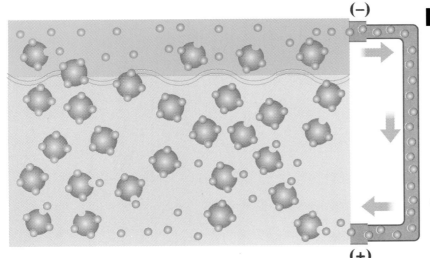

(−)

(+)

Circuit

How an Active Solar Hot Water System Works

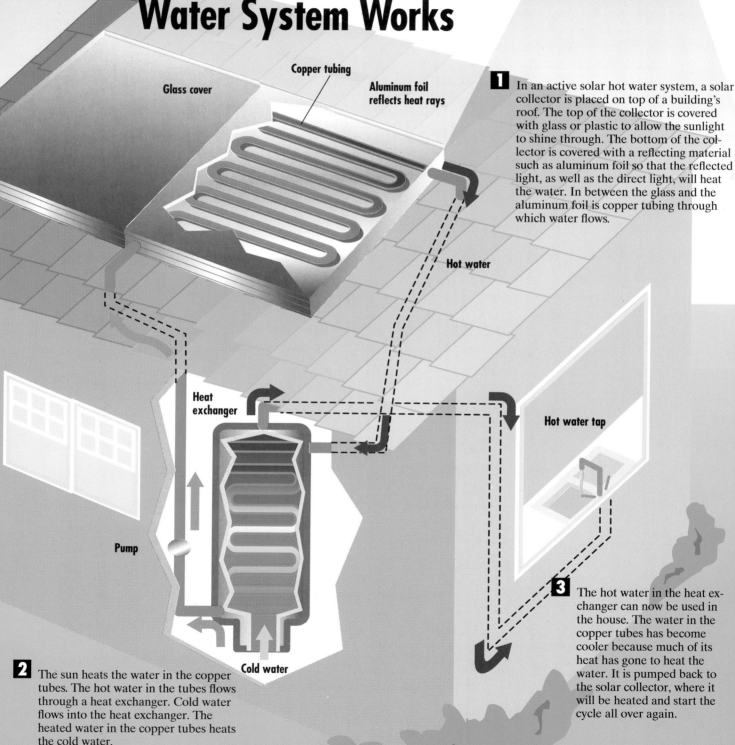

Glass cover

Copper tubing

Aluminum foil reflects heat rays

1 In an active solar hot water system, a solar collector is placed on top of a building's roof. The top of the collector is covered with glass or plastic to allow the sunlight to shine through. The bottom of the collector is covered with a reflecting material such as aluminum foil so that the reflected light, as well as the direct light, will heat the water. In between the glass and the aluminum foil is copper tubing through which water flows.

Hot water

Heat exchanger

Hot water tap

Pump

Cold water

2 The sun heats the water in the copper tubes. The hot water in the tubes flows through a heat exchanger. Cold water flows into the heat exchanger. The heated water in the copper tubes heats the cold water.

3 The hot water in the heat exchanger can now be used in the house. The water in the copper tubes has become cooler because much of its heat has gone to heat the water. It is pumped back to the solar collector, where it will be heated and start the cycle all over again.

How Passive Solar Heating Works

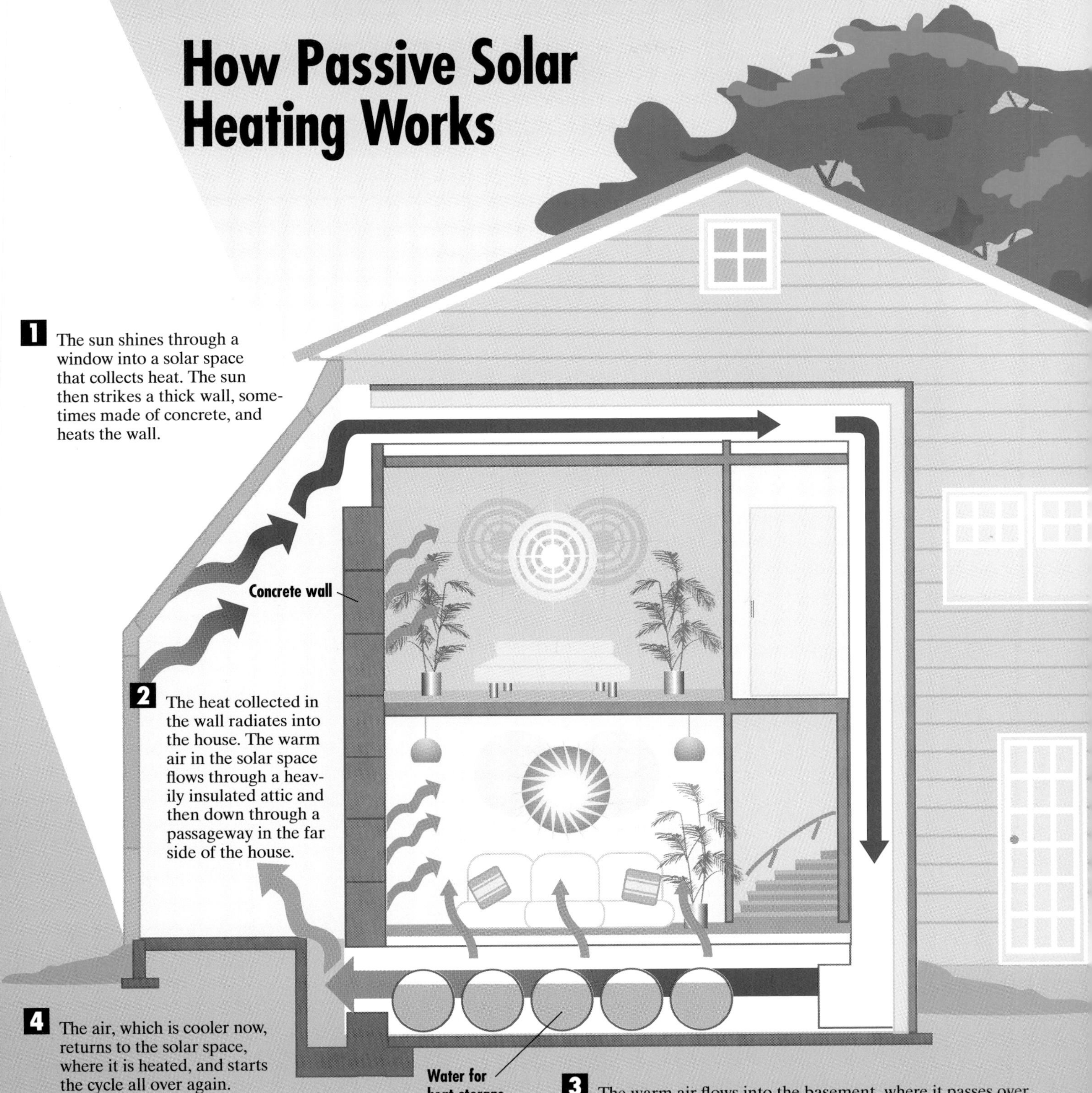

1 The sun shines through a window into a solar space that collects heat. The sun then strikes a thick wall, sometimes made of concrete, and heats the wall.

Concrete wall

2 The heat collected in the wall radiates into the house. The warm air in the solar space flows through a heavily insulated attic and then down through a passageway in the far side of the house.

4 The air, which is cooler now, returns to the solar space, where it is heated, and starts the cycle all over again.

Water for heat storage

3 The warm air flows into the basement, where it passes over water containers. As the warm air flows over the water, the water absorbs and stores heat. The heat then radiates upward through the floors of the house whenever household temperatures fall below that of the water in the containers.

How an Electricity-Producing Windmill Works

Windmills were first invented in Persia in the fifth century A.D. They were used to pump water for irrigation. The basic mechanics of a windmill have not changed since then: The wind strikes a sail or blade and turns it. The moving sail then turns a shaft, which powers a pump, a grindstone, or in more recent times, an electric generator, in which case the windmill is often referred to as a wind turbine. Wind turbines work best when the average wind speed is at least 13 miles per hour.

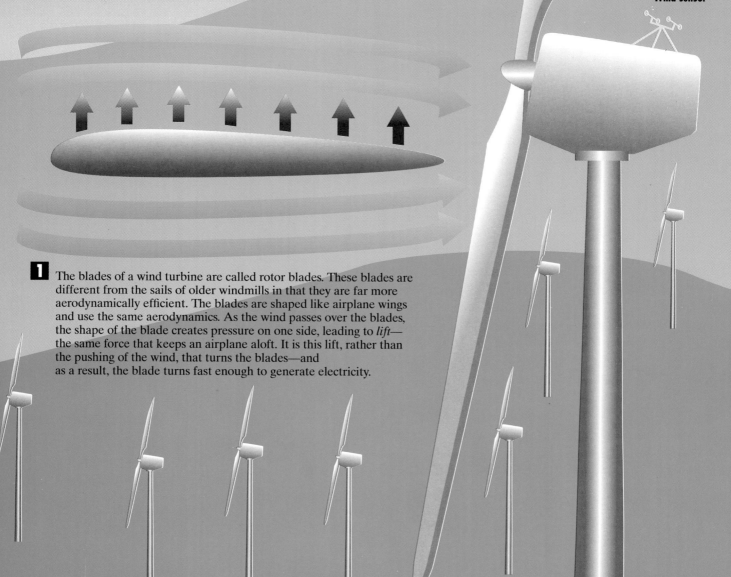

Wind sensor

1 The blades of a wind turbine are called rotor blades. These blades are different from the sails of older windmills in that they are far more aerodynamically efficient. The blades are shaped like airplane wings and use the same aerodynamics. As the wind passes over the blades, the shape of the blade creates pressure on one side, leading to *lift*—the same force that keeps an airplane aloft. It is this lift, rather than the pushing of the wind, that turns the blades—and as a result, the blade turns fast enough to generate electricity.

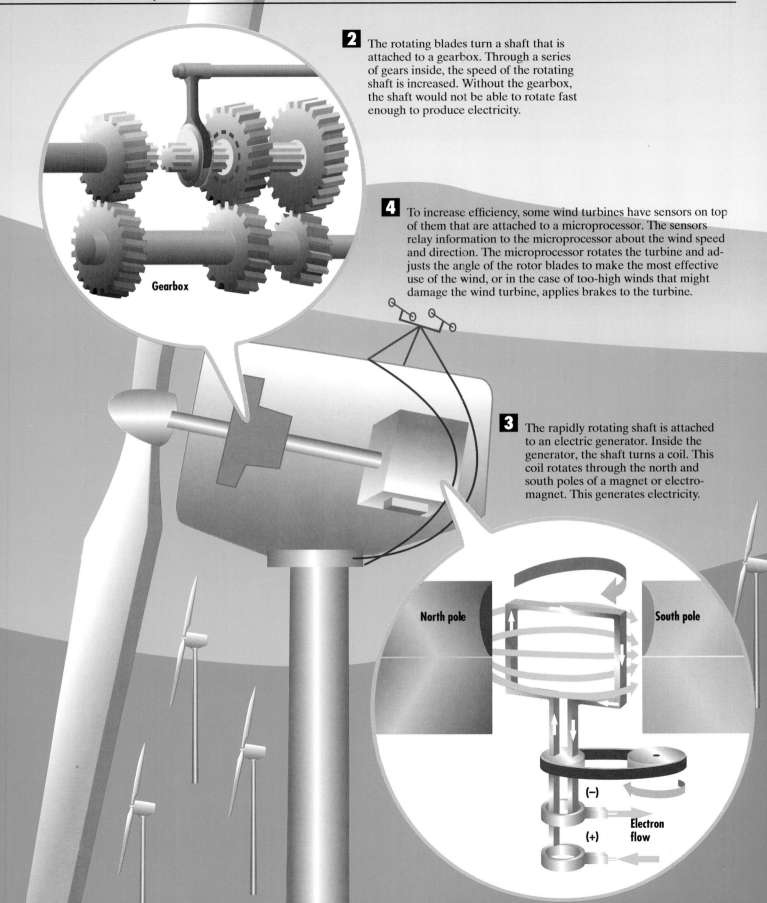

2 The rotating blades turn a shaft that is attached to a gearbox. Through a series of gears inside, the speed of the rotating shaft is increased. Without the gearbox, the shaft would not be able to rotate fast enough to produce electricity.

Gearbox

4 To increase efficiency, some wind turbines have sensors on top of them that are attached to a microprocessor. The sensors relay information to the microprocessor about the wind speed and direction. The microprocessor rotates the turbine and adjusts the angle of the rotor blades to make the most effective use of the wind, or in the case of too-high winds that might damage the wind turbine, applies brakes to the turbine.

3 The rapidly rotating shaft is attached to an electric generator. Inside the generator, the shaft turns a coil. This coil rotates through the north and south poles of a magnet or electromagnet. This generates electricity.

North pole

South pole

(−)

(+)

Electron flow

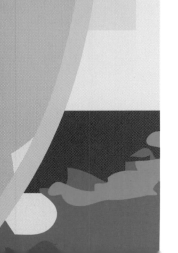

THE ECOLOGY OF MAN-MADE ENVIRONMENTS

CONTENTS

WHEN ONE THINKS of the environment, one thinks of fields, forests, and grassland; oceans, lakes, and rivers. The word *environment* connotes the natural world, not the one made by humankind.

The truth is that civilization—the world we have created over the last several thousand years—has its own living environment as well. But "the environment" is not something "out there," separate from us. Cities and suburbs are subject to the same rules of chemistry, biology, and ecology as is the tropical rain forest or the coral reef.

This final part of the book will explore ways in which cities and suburbs conform to those rules. It will also show that our cities and suburbs, just like our forests and oceans, have natural wonders. In fact, a few varieties of birds are now adapted to living in the city while the rural areas where they originated are rapidly disappearing. The unique concrete canyons of the cities are an acceptable environment for some once-rural animals such as hawks, owls, and even the endangered peregrine falcon.

Increasingly, environmentalists are looking not only to the natural world to understand ecological dangers, but also to where we live and work. A surprising amount of pollution is found not just in our rivers, streams, air, and land, but right in our homes and workplaces. Most of us face more dangers from chemicals such as pesticides at home than we do anywhere else. A lot of the buildings in which we work and study are polluted and unhealthy as well. This condition is referred to as the *sick building syndrome*. This section discusses some of the ways in which a "sick" building can be cured.

Electromagnetic fields may also be evidence of the dark side of civilization. This is an especially controversial and sensitive issue. There are many who believe that the fields cause no harm at all, while others say they can lead to brain cancer, leukemia, and other diseases. This section covers how the electromagnetic fields are created, and explains a theory of how the fields might cause disease.

The genetic engineering of our food is an equally controversial issue. Food companies now have it within their power to alter the basic genetic makeup of fruits, plants, and vegetables. While there are ways in which this technology may be put to good use, there are potential dangers as well. Some people believe that genetically engineered plants may cause dangerous side effects such as allergic reactions. And they say it's possible that the genetically engineered strain could cross-breed with wild plants and create a kind of superpest that could endanger agriculture. We'll examine these issues, and we'll see how the first genetically engineered food to go on the market—the Flavr Savr tomato—was created.

This final section of the book should show how intimately tied to the natural world we are, no matter how we try to shield ourselves or ignore it. We are part of nature and subject to its natural laws as is any other plant or animal. Recognizing that is a large first step toward treating the environment with the respect and care it deserves—and realizing that in the long run it's ourselves, as much as the biosphere, that we help when we treat it that way.

The Sick Building Syndrome

THE AIR IN the building where you work may be making you sick. The Environmental Protection Agency (EPA) has declared that indoor air pollution ranks among the four worst environmental problems we face. The Occupational Safety and Health Administration (OSHA) has estimated that the so-called *sick building syndrome* costs approximately $150 million in lost work time every year because of sickness those buildings cause.

Ironically, the syndrome has its roots in environmentally conscious actions. In the 1970s, when the OPEC nations boycotted the United States by refusing to export oil to it, energy prices skyrocketed and the entire nation began looking for ways to save energy. One way was to construct airtight buildings that hold in the heat in winter and the cool air-conditioned air in summer. These buildings don't allow air to pass between the inside and outside of the building. Because of this, when pollutants are released inside the building, such as formaldehyde from synthetic carpets, they get no chance to dissipate into the outside air. Instead, they build up inside.

Since outside air doesn't circulate inside the building, there is more of a chance that mold and mildew will result, especially in air-conditioning ducts and air-circulation systems. The mold and mildew can cause allergic reactions and hayfeverlike symptoms.

Occasionally, workers in sick buildings face an even greater danger: pesticide poisoning. When pesticides are sprayed to eradicate insect pests and there is improper ventilation, the pesticide fumes stay in the building.

Typically, when a building is sick, people who work in it display a variety of symptoms. Lower respiratory tract infections, irritations of the upper respiratory system and the eyes and nose, and flulike or hayfeverlike complaints are the most common. But other problems such as headaches, nausea, lassitude, chronic complaints of sickness, blurry vision, and skin rashes can occur as well. Some people even worry that long-term exposure to some of the chemicals that cause the sick building syndrome may have even longer-lasting effects, such as causing cancer.

Prevention is generally better than cure. Properly maintaining heating, air-conditioning, and ventilation systems, and making sure there is sufficient fresh air flowing into the building will most likely ensure that a building will not become sick. Regular cleaning of humidifiers and air conditioners will prevent mold and mildew from growing there. Once a building becomes sick, similar actions, as well as removing sources of pollution, such as synthetic carpeting, will generally solve the problem.

How the Sick Building Syndrome Is Caused

Sick building syndrome is a catchall name for what happens when pollutants and irritants inside a building cause any of a variety of health problems to its occupants, such as irritations of the eyes, nose, and throat; nausea; allergic reactions; and flulike symptoms. The Environmental Protection Agency (EPA) estimates that 30% of all buildings and homes in the United States contain enough pollutants to affect people's health.

Many buildings erected or rehabilitated since the 1970s are extremely airtight—so much so that many of them do not even have windows that can be opened. These buildings were designed to save energy, so that heat and air-conditioned air would not escape from them. But this means that indoor pollutants have no chance of dissipating into the outside air, so instead they build up inside. It also means that humidity and moisture tend to stay trapped in the building, leading to the growth of mold and mildew, which commonly cause allergic reactions.

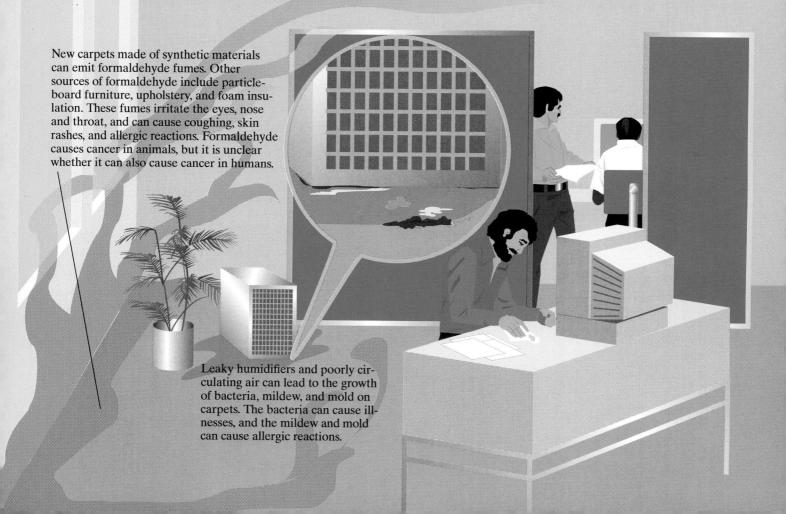

New carpets made of synthetic materials can emit formaldehyde fumes. Other sources of formaldehyde include particle-board furniture, upholstery, and foam insulation. These fumes irritate the eyes, nose and throat, and can cause coughing, skin rashes, and allergic reactions. Formaldehyde causes cancer in animals, but it is unclear whether it can also cause cancer in humans.

Leaky humidifiers and poorly circulating air can lead to the growth of bacteria, mildew, and mold on carpets. The bacteria can cause illnesses, and the mildew and mold can cause allergic reactions.

Aspergillus niger, the microorganism that turns bathroom tiles black, can infect air-conditioning ducts and cause sick building syndrome. This microorganism reproduces by producing tiny spores. These spores are breathed into the lungs. When someone is frequently exposed to these spores, a sensitivity develops, and the person's body produces compounds called histamines whenever the spore is encountered. These histamines cause upper respiratory congestion, runny nose, and a hayfever-like reaction.

Tobacco smoke is a major indoor pollutant, and especially in airtight buildings where the smoke does not dissipate, it can add to the problems caused by sick building syndrome. Tobacco smoke contains over 4,700 compounds, including formaldehyde, ammonia, toluene, sulfur dioxide, and phenol, as well as many toxins, carcinogens and mutagens—material that can cause genetic damage. In addition to causing respiratory problems, this secondhand smoke also increases the risk of lung cancer, it may be a risk factor for heart disease, and it increases the chance that children will get pneumonia and bronchitis.

Home-Based Ecology

MANY OF US live in houses and apartment buildings, in cities and suburbs. Like the sick building syndrome, which was discussed in Chapter 29, our homes also present certain dangers to our indoor environment. To get a sense of the kinds of hazardous chemicals in the home, take this one simple test: Look underneath the sink, or wherever you store your normal household chemicals such as oven and drain cleaners, detergents, and bug sprays. Now read the ingredients—or better yet, the warnings. Each time you use these chemicals, you may be polluting your own indoor atmosphere. And when you don't dispose of them properly, you are certainly polluting the environment.

Houses are subject to other kinds of pollution as well. Lead pipes or solder contaminates drinking water. Asbestos and carbon monoxide can contaminate the air.

In addition, backyard ecosystems are no different than other types of ecosystems in that they are affected by the water, carbon, oxygen, and nitrogen cycles as is the rest of the biosphere. They even have their own food webs as well. Yards are often lush, green places filled with life—from the insects, bacteria, and worms in the soil to the birds nesting in the trees. In fact, the wildlife and plant life in suburban backyards amply augments that found in the wilderness.

However, suburban backyards tend to have only a few species of animals living in them, because the wild brush, natural ponds, and other natural habitats that house many different types of animals have been destroyed or removed from them. Yards favor opportunistic species that can eat a wide variety of foods, and those that have learned, like the raccoon, how to get our food wherever they can, such as by overturning garbage cans.

Our well-tended yards are often islands of peace. Bluejays and squirrels are common cohabitants. Allowing brush to grow or a pond to form may invite other types of animals to move in as well.

Pollution Found in the Home

Asbestos

Formaldehyde is released by synthetic carpets, insulation, drapery, and furniture made from plywood and particle board, among other sources. It causes cancer in animals, but it is unclear if it is carcinogenic to humans. It can, though, irritate the eyes, nose, and throat, and lead to coughing and a variety of allergic reactions.

Pesticides and other agricultural chemicals don't only affect farm workers—people can be poisoned by pesticides at home. The EPA estimates that 121 million pounds of pesticides are used in America's homes and gardens each year. Pesticides can cause short-term illnesses, and have also been linked to cancer and other serious health problems.

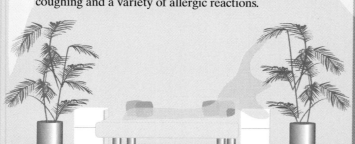

CO

A wide variety of common household products, such as oven cleaners, toilet and drain cleaners, furniture polish, household cleaners, and caulking include many kinds of potentially dangerous chemicals. For example, one of the many chemicals found in paint is methylene chloride, which the U.S. Consumer Product Safety Commission says is a potential carcinogen.

CO

Radon

Radon, an invisible, radioactive gas with no smell, is an especially dangerous household pollutant. Radon is the second leading cause of lung cancer in the United States, after cigarette smoke. It can be found in many kinds of rocks and soil. Granite and black shale have particularly high radon concentrations, so areas with these kinds of rocks, such as the Northeastern United States, are more prone to radon pollution. Radon leaks into a building's basement through cracks in its foundation, and from the basement makes its way into the rest of the house.

Granite

Radon

Asbestos is a known carcinogen that was used in older houses for insulating hot water pipes and as a component in ceiling and floor tile and house siding. Asbestos is less dangerous in tile and siding than it is in other areas. This is because it is locked into the tile and siding and isn't released in the air. But when it is chipped or abraded during normal wear and tear or remodeling, asbestos becomes more hazardous. When asbestos has been sprayed on as insulation, it is easily released into the air as minute fibers, which lodge in the lungs and can cause lung cancer. Spray-on asbestos should be either removed or encapsulated so that it cannot be released into the air.

The toxic heavy metal lead can be found in paint in older houses, in old plumbing, and also in solder for copper pipes. When water corrodes the pipe or solder, the lead is released into the water, which people then drink. Soft water (water with few dissolved minerals) has more of these problems than does hard water, which tends to form mineral deposits on the pipes, forming a barrier between water and the lead.

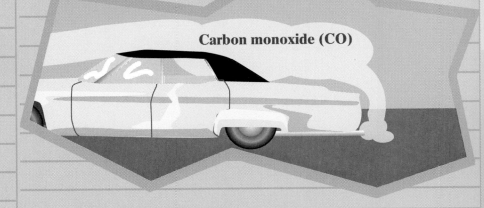

Carbon monoxide (CO)

Pollutants that are created by combustion are a major source of household pollution. Sulfur oxides, nitrogen oxides, and hydrocarbons are examples of these. They are released into the home when a furnace or wood stove is operating improperly, or when an automobile runs in an attached garage. These pollutants irritate the eyes, nose, and throat, and can cause headaches, lethargy, and dizziness, among other health problems. Extreme or excessive concentrations of carbon monoxide are deadly: Hundreds of people die every year in the United States from carbon monoxide poisoning.

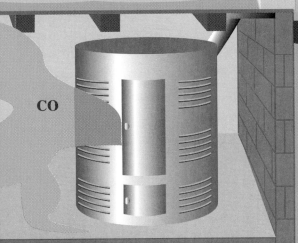

Granite

The Ecology of Backyards

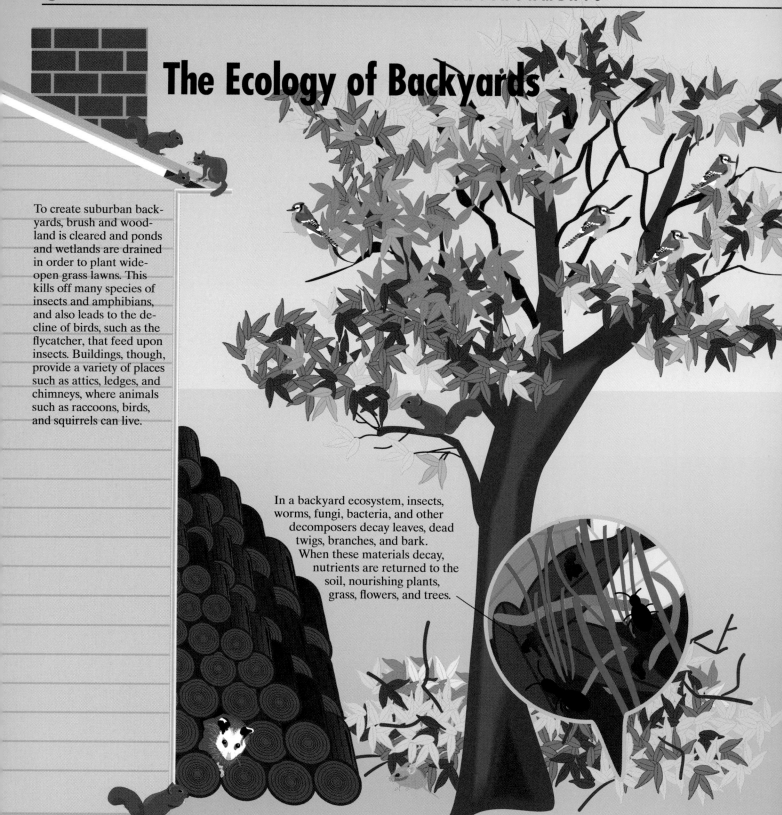

To create suburban backyards, brush and woodland is cleared and ponds and wetlands are drained in order to plant wide-open grass lawns. This kills off many species of insects and amphibians, and also leads to the decline of birds, such as the flycatcher, that feed upon insects. Buildings, though, provide a variety of places such as attics, ledges, and chimneys, where animals such as raccoons, birds, and squirrels can live.

In a backyard ecosystem, insects, worms, fungi, bacteria, and other decomposers decay leaves, dead twigs, branches, and bark. When these materials decay, nutrients are returned to the soil, nourishing plants, grass, flowers, and trees.

Trees and plants prevent erosion because their roots bind the soil together. They provide shade for animals, absorb carbon dioxide and release oxygen into the air, and provide food and a place to live for birds and insects. Trees even clean the air of pollutants.

A sizable number of birds make their homes in suburban backyards because of the easy availability of food from gardens, bird feeders, and garbage cans. However, while the total number of birds in backyards is quite large, the number of species is quite small when compared with the varieties in the wild. Backyards are favorable to birds such as crows and bluejays that are most adaptable to various habitats and will eat a variety of foods.

Backyards are favorable to "opportunistic" species of mammals, which are omnivorous, will eat many different kinds of food, and can live in a variety of ecological niches. Raccoons, for example, are frequent visitors to suburban backyards because they eat refuse from garbage cans.

Large mammals such as bears can be found in some suburban areas. Large predators such as mountain lions and coyotes can also be found in these areas. Increasingly, suburbs are being built in recently wild areas where these types of animals naturally live. Additionally, there is much food available for these animals in the suburbs. Bears, for example, will forage through garbage cans, and predators such as mountain lions will kill and eat raccoons and other suburban animals, including domestic dogs and cats.

CHAPTER 31

The Urban Wild

MODERN-DAY CITIES are a world apart from the wilderness and forests. These islands of asphalt, steel, concrete, and automobiles seem to have nothing of nature in them: Even the polluted air itself is, to a great extent, man-made.

Oddly enough, though, cities teem with wildlife. This wildlife consists of more than rats, pigeons, and squirrels and it exists on more than a few spots of green in city parks. Rare, endangered species such as the peregrine falcon have migrated to cities, as have several species of hawks, owls, and exotic parakeets. Even coyotes have even been seen in some cities.

This happens because, even in cities, the rules of nature apply. The same vast water and chemical cycles that rule the rest of the world rule cities as well. And the city, just like the most isolated rain forest in the world, has its own food web in which all creatures play a part.

Probably the most dramatic new wild visitor to cities is the peregrine falcon, a predator and endangered species. Biologists have released these birds into several North American cities, and surprisingly, the falcon has thrived. It rides the air currents high above the city as it normally rides air currents near cliffs. It nests on the ledges of skyscrapers as it nests on cliff edges. And it feeds on birds such as pigeons and starlings as it feeds on other birds in the wild. Hawks and owls have come to the cities as well, to feed on squirrels and rodents.

In the desert city of Tucson, Arizona, rare bird species normally found in the desert are increasingly becoming urban dwellers as the city expands. They are attracted by the grass and weeds in the city, and are attempting to adapt to the expansion of the city into their habitat.

Other kinds of birds have an even more complex urban life. In some cities, for example, starlings sleep in buildings in the urban core. In the daytime, they fly to outlying farm areas to feed on grain.

Not all urban wildlife is welcome, though. Wild dog packs have started to roam in some of the more devastated parts of cities. Stray dogs breed and their feral offspring congregate into packs, where they live off of garbage and other refuse.

Still, most wildlife in the city is a welcome reminder that no matter where we live, even in the tallest concrete canyon, nature is still with us.

A Walk on the Wild Side: Wildlife in the City

Cities are made up of more than just steel, concrete, and glass. Many animals make their home there because the city is as much of an environment as any other place on earth. Species such as falcons, hawks, and even exotic birds that normally live in the wilderness sometimes find urban homes.

The peregrine falcon, an endangered species, has found safe homes in surprising places: North American cities. Biologists released the falcons into the cities in the hope that they would find safe harbor there and so help save the species from extinction. The experiment worked. Peregrine falcons make their homes atop skyscrapers, which resemble their natural rocky cliff homes, and they ride the air currents atop the city in search of prey. The falcons eat birds such as pigeons and starlings.

The red-tailed hawk also has been known to live in urban areas. Some hawks have wintered in the Boston Common and Public Garden, feeding on squirrels and rodents. When the warm weather returns in the spring, they migrate north. They also live in other cities, such as Los Angeles.

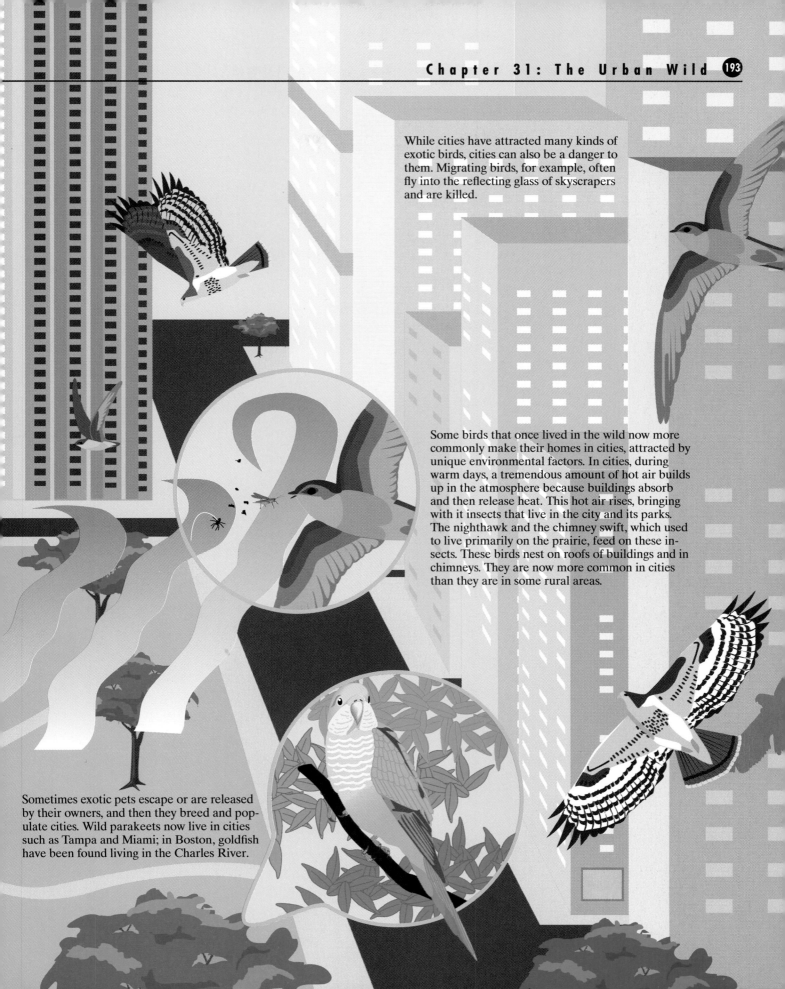

While cities have attracted many kinds of exotic birds, cities can also be a danger to them. Migrating birds, for example, often fly into the reflecting glass of skyscrapers and are killed.

Some birds that once lived in the wild now more commonly make their homes in cities, attracted by unique environmental factors. In cities, during warm days, a tremendous amount of hot air builds up in the atmosphere because buildings absorb and then release heat. This hot air rises, bringing with it insects that live in the city and its parks. The nighthawk and the chimney swift, which used to live primarily on the prairie, feed on these insects. These birds nest on roofs of buildings and in chimneys. They are now more common in cities than they are in some rural areas.

Sometimes exotic pets escape or are released by their owners, and then they breed and populate cities. Wild parakeets now live in cities such as Tampa and Miami; in Boston, goldfish have been found living in the Charles River.

CHAPTER
32

The Dangers of Electromagnetic Fields

WE ARE SURROUNDED by electricity. The homes we live in, the buildings we work in—everywhere we go, invisible electric currents are flowing through appliances, lightbulbs, and power lines. This electricity is called alternating current, or AC, electricity, because the current changes direction, or alternates, many times a second. It switches direction 60 times a second, and so is referred to as 60 hertz (Hz), an extremely low frequency.

All electric currents cause *electromagnetic fields*—invisible fields that carry energy. The electricity we use in our homes causes extremely low frequency (ELF) fields. These fields are very weak—so weak that they vanish inches or feet away from an appliance—because the currents that cause them are weak. So we are not exposed to them constantly, and in any event, they have little energy.

However, there are places where ELF fields are extremely strong. High-voltage power lines and electricity distribution substations give off powerful electromagnetic fields.

Some houses and schools are located near high-voltage power lines and electricity substations. This means the people living in the homes or working or studying in the schools are subject to these more powerful electromagnetic fields for many hours a day. And therein lies the controversy.

At some schools and in some neighborhoods located near these lines and substations, extremely high incidences of brain cancer, leukemia, and other forms of cancer have been found. For example, a single street located near a substation in Guilford, Connecticut had practically an epidemic level of cases of brain cancer. And across the country in Montecito, California, many children in a single school were stricken with leukemia and lymphoma—the school was located near a substation and an electric transmission line cut across the school grounds.

Some scientists and power company officials say that outbreaks like these are pure coincidence and that statistically, such cases are bound to occur. There is no evidence, they say, to prove that ELF fields cause disease. Other scientists, as well as some parents and neighbors, feel certain that the electric lines and substations are the cause of the problems. They say that ELF fields alter brain chemistry, promote the growth of tumors, and weaken the body's immune system.

At the moment, neither side can convince the other. It is a case, though, where prudence should prevail: High-voltage lines and substations should be located away from schools and homes.

The Possible Hazards of Electromagnetic Fields

There is a great deal of controversy over whether electromagnetic fields cause diseases such as cancer and leukemia. While ionizing radiation is known to cause cancer, it is unclear whether electromagnetic radiation caused by electricity can. However, a number of studies have shown that there is a link.

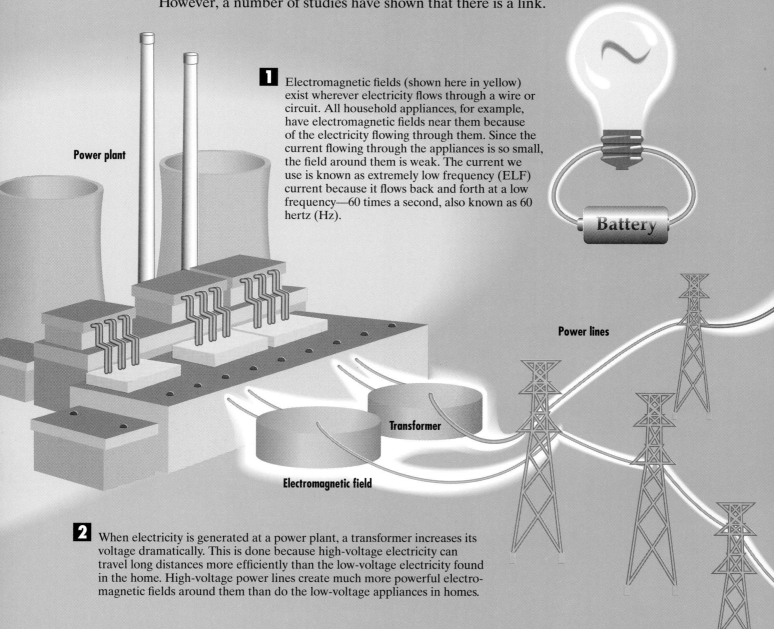

1 Electromagnetic fields (shown here in yellow) exist wherever electricity flows through a wire or circuit. All household appliances, for example, have electromagnetic fields near them because of the electricity flowing through them. Since the current flowing through the appliances is so small, the field around them is weak. The current we use is known as extremely low frequency (ELF) current because it flows back and forth at a low frequency—60 times a second, also known as 60 hertz (Hz).

Power plant

Battery

Power lines

Transformer

Electromagnetic field

2 When electricity is generated at a power plant, a transformer increases its voltage dramatically. This is done because high-voltage electricity can travel long distances more efficiently than the low-voltage electricity found in the home. High-voltage power lines create much more powerful electromagnetic fields around them than do the low-voltage appliances in homes.

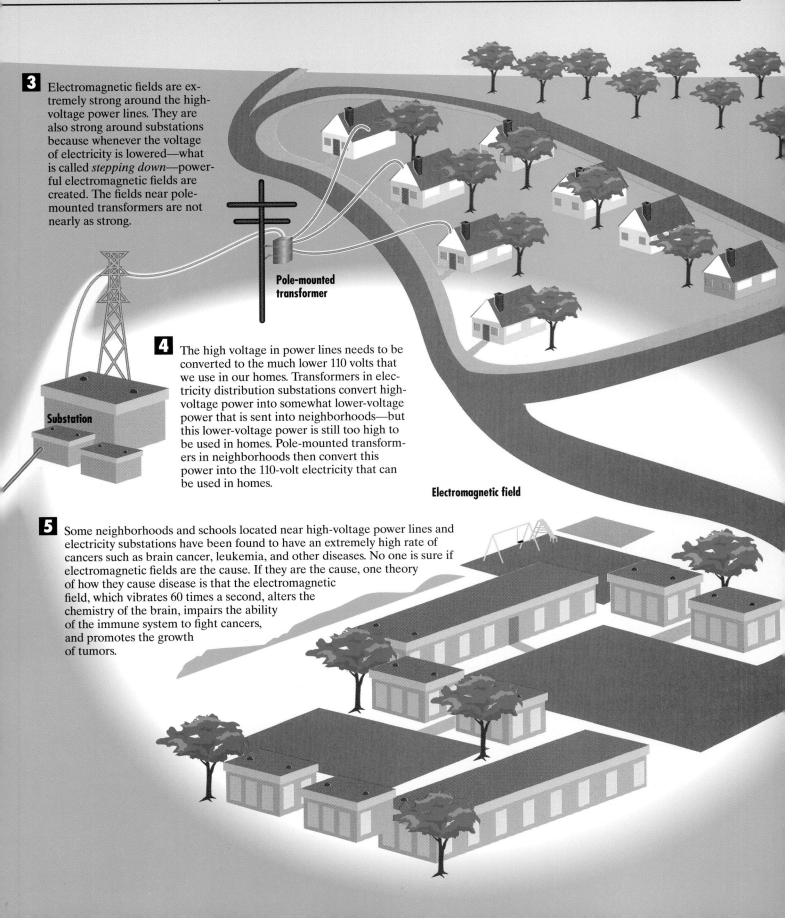

3 Electromagnetic fields are extremely strong around the high-voltage power lines. They are also strong around substations because whenever the voltage of electricity is lowered—what is called *stepping down*—powerful electromagnetic fields are created. The fields near pole-mounted transformers are not nearly as strong.

Pole-mounted transformer

Substation

4 The high voltage in power lines needs to be converted to the much lower 110 volts that we use in our homes. Transformers in electricity distribution substations convert high-voltage power into somewhat lower-voltage power that is sent into neighborhoods—but this lower-voltage power is still too high to be used in homes. Pole-mounted transformers in neighborhoods then convert this power into the 110-volt electricity that can be used in homes.

Electromagnetic field

5 Some neighborhoods and schools located near high-voltage power lines and electricity substations have been found to have an extremely high rate of cancers such as brain cancer, leukemia, and other diseases. No one is sure if electromagnetic fields are the cause. If they are the cause, one theory of how they cause disease is that the electromagnetic field, which vibrates 60 times a second, alters the chemistry of the brain, impairs the ability of the immune system to fight cancers, and promotes the growth of tumors.

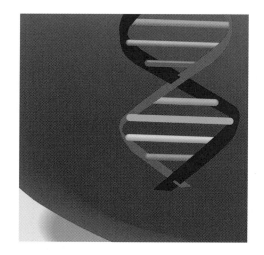

CHAPTER 33

The Controversial Green Revolution: Genetically Engineered Crops

WE NOW HAVE it within our power to alter the most basic makeup of the plants and foods we use and eat. Through genetic engineering, we are able to manipulate the most basic structures of life—the genetic material that defines life itself. Plants are genetically engineered when a gene from one plant or animal, or a new gene created by scientists, is put into another plant to make improvements, such as resistance to frost. This particular enhancement may be accomplished by taking the gene from the Arctic cod and implanting it into a vegetable.

In 1994, the first genetically engineered food hit store shelves across the country—the Flavr Savr tomato, which resists softening and rotting. It can be ripened on the vine instead of by using chemicals, and so should taste superior to normal supermarket fare.

The long-term impact of genetic engineering on the environment is unclear. Those who favor the practice say that it can bring untold benefits. They feel that foods can be engineered to resist disease and pests—that plants can create their own natural pesticides, eliminating the need for the millions of tons of pesticides that are sprayed every year. Others feel that these potential benefits are unlikely. There is even a push to engineer plants that tolerate higher levels of herbicides. Proponents of genetic engineering also feel that they can make it easier to feed more people in the world. In addition, more nutritious and more flavorful foods will be created.

On the other side are those who maintain that more caution is necessary before allowing genetically engineered plants—what some call "Frankenfoods"—to be in wide use. They note that such foods may have harmful side effects or create long-term health hazards, and that more testing needs to be done. They believe that a gene from a food that often produces allergies, such as a peanut, could be put into a food such as a tomato, and that unsuspecting people with peanut allergies could eat the tomato and face severe health consequences. They add that genetically engineered foods may cross-breed with plants in the wild and create plants that could become serious pests.

We have always manipulated the genes of plants to give them attributes that we want, through breeding and cross-breeding. Genetic engineering, though, gives us an extraordinarily new power to do this. Only time will tell whether that power will be good or bad for the environment and consumers.

How the Flavr Savr Tomato Was Genetically Engineered

Ethylene gas

1 Supermarket tomatoes generally have little taste because they are picked while they are green, before they become ripe. That's because once a tomato becomes ripe on the vine, it quickly softens and rots before it can be shipped to market. So growers pick the tomatoes while the fruit is still green, then expose them to ethylene gas. The gas turns the skin red and, to a certain extent, ripens the tomato—but it still does not taste nearly as good as a vine-ripened tomato.

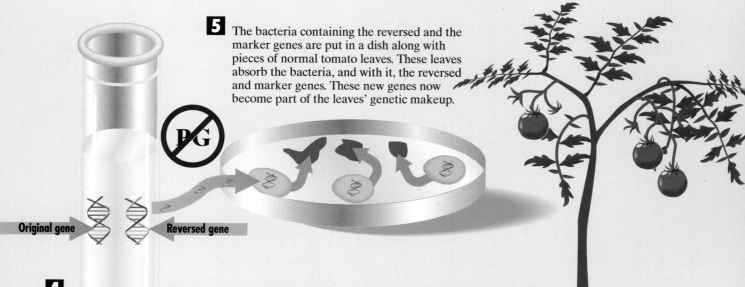

5 The bacteria containing the reversed and the marker genes are put in a dish along with pieces of normal tomato leaves. These leaves absorb the bacteria, and with it, the reversed and marker genes. These new genes now become part of the leaves' genetic makeup.

Original gene

Reversed gene

4 The gene was then reversed by bioengineers. This reversed gene will not tell the tomato's cells to produce PG. The gene was placed in bacteria, along with a marker gene that is easy to detect and allows scientists to know whether the reversed gene has been placed in the tomato DNA properly.

6 The pieces of leaf are sprouted and then planted. They are allowed to become full-grown plants. Seeds from these genetically altered tomatoes are harvested and then planted.

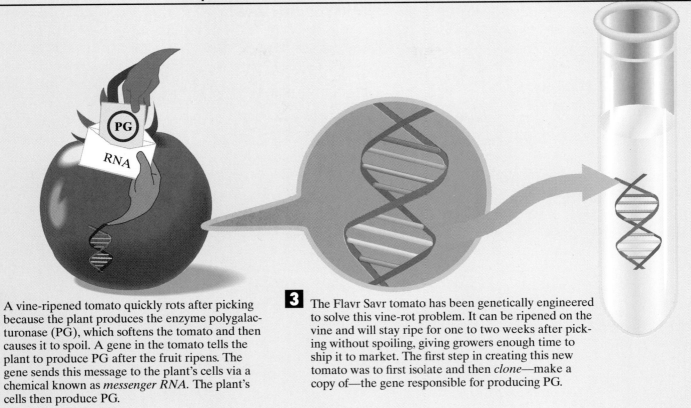

2 A vine-ripened tomato quickly rots after picking because the plant produces the enzyme polygalacturonase (PG), which softens the tomato and then causes it to spoil. A gene in the tomato tells the plant to produce PG after the fruit ripens. The gene sends this message to the plant's cells via a chemical known as *messenger RNA*. The plant's cells then produce PG.

3 The Flavr Savr tomato has been genetically engineered to solve this vine-rot problem. It can be ripened on the vine and will stay ripe for one to two weeks after picking without spoiling, giving growers enough time to ship it to market. The first step in creating this new tomato was to first isolate and then *clone*—make a copy of—the gene responsible for producing PG.

7 The tomatoes produced by these seeds do not soften and rot quickly after they ripen because the reversed gene produces a kind of messenger RNA that interferes with the ability of the normal gene's RNA to tell the plant's cells to produce PG. Farmers can now allow the tomatoes to ripen on the vine because they can be shipped to supermarkets before they spoil.

ATTENTION TEACHERS AND TRAINERS
Now You Can Teach From These Books!

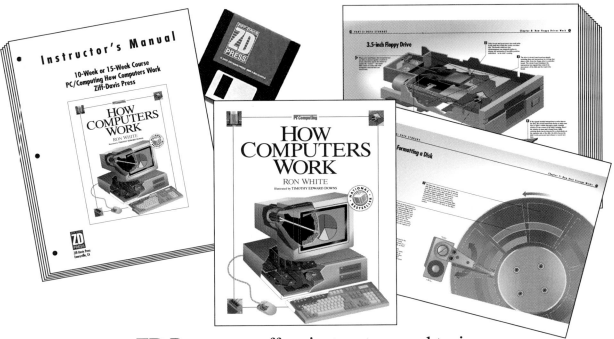

ZD Press now offers instructors and trainers
the materials they need to use these books in their classes.

- An Instructor's Manual features flexible lessons designed for use in a 10- or 15-week course (30-45 course hours).

- Student exercises and tests on floppy disk provide you with an easy way to tailor and/or duplicate tests as you need them.

- A Transparency Package contains all the graphics from the book, each on a single, full-color transparency.

- Spanish edition of *PC/Computing How Computers Work* will be available.

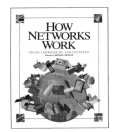
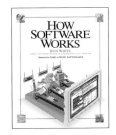

ZIFF-DAVIS
ZD
PRESS

Imagination
INNOVATION·INSIGHT

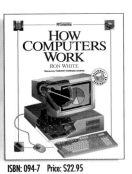

How Computers Work
RON WHITE

ISBN: 094-7   Price: $22.95
Also available in Spanish.

No other books bring computer technology to life like the HOW IT WORKS series from Ziff-Davis Press. Lavish, full-color illustrations and lucid text from some of the world's top computer commentators make HOW IT WORKS books an exciting way to explore the inner workings of PC technology.

PC Computing

HOW COMPUTERS WORK

INCLUDES INTERACTIVE CD-ROM

RON WHITE
Illustrated by T

ISBN: 250-8   Price: $39.95

intel
HOW MICROPROCESSORS WORK
GREGG WYANT AND TUCKER HAMMERSTROM
Illustrated by K. DANIEL CLARK

ISBN: 145-5
Price: $24.95

HOW DESKTOP PUBLISHING WORKS
PAMELA PFIFFNER AND BRUCE FRASER

ISBN: 191-9
Price: $24.95

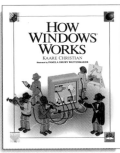

HOW WINDOWS WORKS
KAARE CHRISTIAN

ISBN: 193-5   Price: $24.95

HOW COMPUTER PROGRAMMING WORKS
DANIEL APPLEMAN

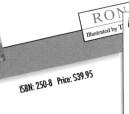

ISBN: 195-1   Price: $24.95

HOW MULTIMEDIA WORKS
ERIK HOLSINGER

ISBN: 208-7   Price: $24.95

HOW THE INTERNET WORKS
JOSHUA EDDINGS

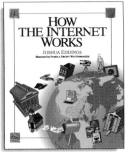

ISBN: 192-7   Price: $24.95

ZIFF-DAVIS ZD PRESS

Available at all fine bookstores or by calling 1-800-688-0448, ext. 100. Call for more information on the Instructor's Supplement, including transparencies for each book in the *How It Works* Series.

© 1994 Ziff-Davis Press

Click, Click,

PC/Computing
How Computers Work
CD-ROM/Book
extravaganza
from
Ziff-Davis Press.

W H I Z

Click your way through an electrifying multimedia voyage to the heart of the computer with *How Multimedia Computers Work*—a unique CD-ROM packaged with the classic best-selling book *PC/Computing How Computers Work.*

In *How Multimedia Computers Work*, fun, fast-paced, fascinating tours of your computer's incredible innards combine state-of-the-art 3D animation with lively dialog and music for a richly interactive sensory feast. Also included are provocative video interviews with well-known computer industry figures—plus tons

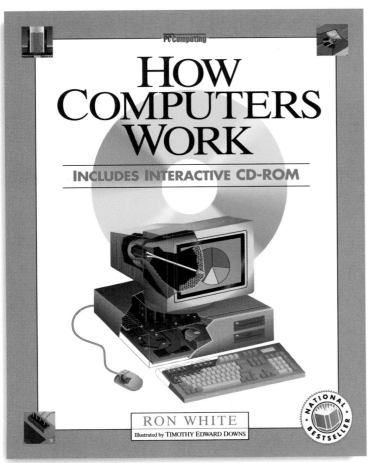

of computing tips from the top authors at Ziff-Davis Press. Teamed up with a book that has already shown legions of computer users what makes their machine tick, *How Multimedia Computers Work*

is a real whiz-bang experience that's sure to make you see your computer in a whole new light.

Ask your favorite bookseller for *PC/Computing How Computers Work* with *How Multimedia Computers Work* on interactive CD-ROM.

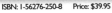
ISBN: 1-56276-250-8   Price: $39.95

BANG

ZIFF-DAVIS
ZD
PRESS

© 1994 Ziff-Davis Press

Ziff-Davis Press books are available at all fine bookstores,
or call 1-800-688-0448, ext. 247.

Ziff-Davis Press Survey of Readers

Please help us in our effort to produce the best books on personal computing.
For your assistance, we would be pleased to send you a FREE catalog
featuring the complete line of Ziff-Davis Press books.

1. How did you first learn about this book?

Recommended by a friend . . . . ☐ -1 (5)

Recommended by store personnel . . . . ☐ -2

Saw in Ziff-Davis Press catalog . . . . ☐ -3

Received advertisement in the mail . . . . ☐ -4

Saw the book on bookshelf at store . . . . ☐ -5

Read book review in: _____ ☐ -6

Saw an advertisement in: _____ ☐ -7

Other (Please specify): _____ ☐ -8

2. Which THREE of the following factors most influenced your decision to purchase this book? (Please check up to THREE.)

Front or back cover information on book . . . ☐ -1 (6)

Logo of magazine affiliated with book . . . . . . ☐ -2

Special approach to the content . . . . ☐ -3

Completeness of content . . . . ☐ -4

Author's reputation. . . . . ☐ -5

Publisher's reputation . . . . ☐ -6

Book cover design or layout . . . . ☐ -7

Index or table of contents of book . . . . ☐ -8

Price of book . . . . ☐ -9

Special effects, graphics, illustrations . . . . . . ☐ -0

Other (Please specify): _____ ☐ -x

3. How many computer books have you purchased in the last six months? _____ (7-10)

4. On a scale of 1 to 5, where 5 is excellent, 4 is above average, 3 is average, 2 is below average, and 1 is poor, please rate each of the following aspects of this book below. (Please circle your answer.)

Depth/completeness of coverage	5	4	3	2	1	(11)
Organization of material	5	4	3	2	1	(12)
Ease of finding topic	5	4	3	2	1	(13)
Special features/time saving tips	5	4	3	2	1	(14)
Appropriate level of writing	5	4	3	2	1	(15)
Usefulness of table of contents	5	4	3	2	1	(16)
Usefulness of index	5	4	3	2	1	(17)
Usefulness of accompanying disk	5	4	3	2	1	(18)
Usefulness of illustrations/graphics	5	4	3	2	1	(19)
Cover design and attractiveness	5	4	3	2	1	(20)
Overall design and layout of book	5	4	3	2	1	(21)
Overall satisfaction with book	5	4	3	2	1	(22)

5. Which of the following computer publications do you read regularly; that is, 3 out of 4 issues?

Byte . . . . ☐ -1 (23)

Computer Shopper . . . . ☐ -2

Corporate Computing . . . . ☐ -3

Dr. Dobb's Journal . . . . ☐ -4

LAN Magazine . . . . ☐ -5

MacWEEK . . . . ☐ -6

MacUser . . . . ☐ -7

PC Computing . . . . ☐ -8

PC Magazine . . . . ☐ -9

PC WEEK . . . . ☐ -0

Windows Sources . . . . ☐ -x

Other (Please specify): _____ ☐ -y

Please turn page.

PLEASE TAPE HERE ONLY—DO NOT STAPLE

6. What is your level of experience with personal computers? With the subject of this book?

	With PCs	With subject of book
Beginner	☐ -1 (24)	☐ -1 (25)
Intermediate	☐ -2	☐ -2
Advanced	☐ -3	☐ -3

7. Which of the following best describes your job title?

Officer (CEO/President/VP/owner)........ ☐ -1 (26)

Director/head......................... ☐ -2

Manager/supervisor.................... ☐ -3

Administration/staff................... ☐ -4

Teacher/educator/trainer.............. ☐ -5

Lawyer/doctor/medical professional....... ☐ -6

Engineer/technician................... ☐ -7

Consultant........................... ☐ -8

Not employed/student/retired........... ☐ -9

Other (Please specify): _____ ☐ -0

8. What is your age?

Under 20............................. ☐ -1 (27)

21-29................................ ☐ -2

30-39................................ ☐ -3

40-49................................ ☐ -4

50-59................................ ☐ -5

60 or over........................... ☐ -6

9. Are you:

Male................................. ☐ -1 (28)

Female............................... ☐ -2

Thank you for your assistance with this important information! Please write your address below to receive our free catalog.

Name: _____

Address: _____

City/State/Zip: _____

Fold here to mail.

2427-13-08

_____

_____

_____

BUSINESS REPLY MAIL
FIRST CLASS MAIL   PERMIT NO. 1612   OAKLAND, CA

POSTAGE WILL BE PAID BY ADDRESSEE

Ziff-Davis Press
5903 Christie Avenue
Emeryville, CA 94608-1925
Attn: Marketing

NO POSTAGE
NECESSARY
IF MAILED IN
THE UNITED
STATES